Christmas '04

We hope this [illegible]
you on your path to
happiness and success

Love you.

Mom & Dad

TEN DEADLY MARKETING SINS

SIGNS AND SOLUTIONS

Published by John Wiley & Sons, Inc., Hoboken, New Jersey.
Published simultaneously in Canada.

For general information on our other products and services please contact our Customer Care Department within the United States at (800) 762-2974, outside the United States at (317) 572-3993 or fax (317) 572-4002.

Wiley also publishes its books in a variety of electronic formats. Some content that appears in print may not be available in electronic books. For more information about Wiley products, visit our web site at www.Wiley.com.

Library of Congress Cataloging-in-Publication Data:

Kotler, Philip.
Ten deadly marketing sins : signs and solutions / Philip Kotler.
p. cm.
ISBN 0-471-65022-6 (cloth)
1. Marketing—Management. I. Title: 10 deadly marketing sins. II. Title.
HF5415.13 .K654 2004
658.8—dc22

2003026035

Printed in the United States of America.

10 9 8 7 6 5 4 3 2 1

I dedicate this book to my six grandchildren—Jordan, Jamie, Ellie, Olivia, Abby, and Sam—whom I love dearly.

Acknowledgments

This book is based on many years of working with consulting firms and individual clients. I would like especially to acknowledge Hamilton Consultants of Cambridge, Massachusetts (www.hamiltonco.com). An original version of the ten most common findings was created by my earlier *Marketing Audit* co-author, Will Rodgers, and his colleagues at the MAC Group and Hamilton Consultants. They based their conclusions on the findings from over 75 marketing audits of business units conducted over a 15-year period. Hamilton has further modified the audit into something they call "Market-based Profit Improvement" wherein they link audit findings to bottom line impact. I used the list of major marketing deficiencies and my own consulting experiences as a springboard for developing this book.

I also want to acknowledge Kotler Marketing Group of Washington, D.C. (www.kotlermarketing.com), for their commitment to identifying major marketing deficiencies and proposing innovative solutions. Kotler Marketing Group focuses on strategic marketing and has worked with such major clients as AT&T, IBM, JP Morgan, Northwestern Mutual, Weyerhaeuser, Baxter, Pfizer, Shell Chemical, Ford, McDonald's, Michelin, and SAS Airlines. Their president and founder, Milton Kotler, has shown an uncanny marketing imagination in bringing fresh "out-of-the-box" thinking to guide company solutions.

Contents

Introduction *The State of Marketing Today* 1

Chapter 1 Your Company Is Not Sufficiently Market Focused and Customer Driven 13

Chapter 2 Your Company Does Not Fully Understand Its Target Customers 29

Chapter 3 Your Company Needs to Better Define and Monitor Its Competitors 43

Chapter 4 Your Company Has Not Properly Managed Its Relationships with Its Stakeholders 53

Chapter 5 Your Company Is Not Good at Finding New Opportunities 63

Chapter 6 Your Company's Marketing Planning Process Is Deficient 73

Chapter 7 Your Company's Product and Service Policies Need Tightening 81

Chapter 8 Your Company's Brand-Building and Communication Skills Are Weak 89

Chapter 9 Your Company Is Not Well Organized to Carry On Effective and Efficient Marketing 103

Chapter 10 Your Company Has Not Made Maximum Use of Technology 129

Epilogue *The Ten Commandments of Marketing Effectiveness* 143

Index 147

Introduction

The State of Marketing Today

Marketing is in bad shape. Not marketing theory, but marketing practice. Every new product or service needs to be supported by a marketing plan that brings in a good return that covers the corresponding investment of time and money. But then why do 75 percent of new products, services, and businesses fail?[1] These failures happen in spite of all the work that goes into market research, concept development and testing, business analysis, product development and testing, market testing, and commercial launch.

Marketing is supposed to drive business strategy. The marketers' job is to *research* new opportunities for the company and carefully apply *segmentation, targeting, and positioning* (STP) to point a new business in the right direction. Then marketers are supposed to flesh out the *4Ps—Product, Price, Place, and Promotion*—making sure that they are consistent with each other and with the STP strategy. Then marketers are supposed to *implement* the plan and *monitor* the results. When the results deviate from the plan, marketers have to decide if the culprit is weak implementation, an incoherent marketing mix, a misdirected STP, or ultimately incompetent market research.

But today, too many marketing departments don't handle this whole process. It's handled by a mix of marketers, strategists, financial types, and operations people. Somehow a new product or service emerges and marketing is left to its true mission as conceived by others in the company, namely selling and promoting. Most of marketing is reduced to a one-P function—Promotion—not a four-P job. Because the company ends up making a product that doesn't sell well, most of marketing's task is to clear up the mess through hard selling and advertising.

Here is an example of one-P marketing. I asked the Marketing Vice President of a major European airline whether he sets the fares on the airline:

> *"Finance does that."*
> *"Do you influence the food served on the airplane?"*
> "No, *that's done by catering."*
> *"Do you have a say in setting the standards for hiring cabin crew?"*
> "No, *human resources handles that."*
> *"What about the cleanliness of the planes?"*
> *"That's maintenance's job."*
> *"Then what do you do?"*
> *"I manage advertising and selling."*

Clearly, this airline is treating marketing as a one-P function.

Worse, marketing isn't handling advertising and selling very well. Ask any CEO who shudders when he gets the advertising bill in a period when sales are flat or down. "What did the advertising do for us?" he asks the Marketing Vice President. At best, the answer is that sales would have been even worse without it. "But as an investment, what did we get back?" And there isn't a good answer.

CEOs are understandably growing impatient with marketing. They feel that they get accountability for their investments in finance, production, information technology, even purchasing, but don't know what their marketing spending is achieving. Granted that marketing involves a more complex chain of events where it is harder to trace cause and effect. But some progress is being made in theory and other companies are putting it into practice. Why can't this happen in their company?

Every sign suggests that marketing will become more challenging in the future. Consider the following:

- National brands are finding it harder to get an adequate premium to cover their brand-building cost. Why? Wal-Mart and its imitators are insisting on much lower prices from suppliers if these suppliers want Wal-Mart's business. And megaretailers are increasingly putting out their own store brands that are reaching a level of quality equal to the national brands. Store brands don't have to pay for research, advertising, and selling. We are hearing that Generation Y is more skeptical of advertising. Naomi Klein and her *No Logo* book is making a lot of people think about how much should they pay for the more advertised brands and what effects rampant branding has on society's costs.[2]

- Companies have been embracing Customer Relationship Management (CRM) as the latest cure for their ills. This means collecting private information about individuals to better guess at what they can be tempted to buy. But there is growing opposition to the collection of personal information. Furthermore, people are increasingly upset with junk mail, e-mail, and phone calls. In fact, Congress passed a law giving people the right to list their households as not available for phone calls, with a penalty of $11,000 for offending companies. Companies better move to permission or "opt-in" marketing as soon as they can.

- Loyalty schemes seem like a good idea and they work well for their first adopters. But their competitors have no choice but to launch their own frequent-buyer schemes. Today, most businesspeople carry Visa, MasterCard, and American Express and they get points whether they fly American, United, or Delta.

- No matter how cheaply a company can produce its product domestically, it can't be the cheapest as long as China has a say. China can produce everything cheaper and is beginning to make it as good. China will have the power to repeat the Japanese game: better quality at lower prices. This has been a blow to countries that would advertise lower cost labor, such as Latin American and eastern European countries. Thus Mexico has been losing auto and other factories in the *mequiladora* area as they move to China. Naturally U.S. producers will transfer domestic sourcing and production to cheaper areas, leading to declines in U.S. employment. Falling employment means less purchasing power and fewer sales, thus producing a vicious circle.

- Mass marketing costs are rising even though mass marketing effectiveness is falling. As fewer people pay attention to TV commercials—either ignoring or zapping them—TV networks are raising their prices. This will force marketers to find more effective media.
- Differentiation has been the marketer's war cry: "Differentiate, differentiate, differentiate." Professor Theodore Levitt said years ago that you can differentiate anything, including salt and cement. But the problem is twofold. Many differentiations don't matter to customers . . . they are spurious or not compelling. Worse, competitors are quick to copy any effective differentiation, leading innovators to enjoy even shorter life cycles, barely recovering their investments.

- Consumers are more informed and sophisticated in their buying habits. Mr. Jones, who wants to buy a Nikon Coolpix 4300 digital camera, goes on www.mysimon.com and finds over 25 online merchants stating their prices for this camera. And the variance is shocking; prices range from $339 to $449! People are being trained into price consciousness. Buying online is all about price, not reliability or service differences. Consider further that today's customers walk into an auto dealership armed with information on exactly what the car should cost them. Some even go on Priceline.com and state what they will pay for such-and-such-a-car if any dealer will accept their offer.
- Companies continue to cut their marketing expenses during recessions, the one prop on which their sales depend. But because the company doesn't get hard data on what their marketing expenditures are doing, can you blame them?

We can go on but the point is well made: Marketers will face increasing challenges in trying to preserve company margins and hit company profit targets. To make matters worse, many companies are inefficiently organized from a marketing point of view. Adding company marketing inefficiency and ineffectiveness to all these challenges is a recipe for disaster.

I set out to identify the most glaring marketing deficiencies that handicap companies from succeeding in the marketplace. I found ten of them that I call *the Ten Deadly Sins of Marketing*. Companies need to consider two things: First, what *signs* would indicate that a company is committing a specific marketing sin? Second, what are the best *solutions* for overcoming this problem?

If I ran a company, I would sit down with my colleagues and examine each of the ten sins. We would determine which are the most serious. We would then determine the best solution to pursue in each case. I would assign a senior executive to be responsible for improving our performance along those lines. I would recognize that some of these deficiencies will require a sustained investment over a long period, but if it is preventing our success in the marketplace, I would support it.

My basic belief is that marketing's work should not be so much about selling but about creating products that don't need selling. Marketing people need the skills of identifying opportunities (i.e., unmet needs or life-enhancing solutions), and developing and implementing plans that succeed in the marketplace. I want marketing to retrieve its true role, that of driving business strategy.

Finally, here are the Ten Deadly Sins of Marketing.[3]

The Ten Deadly Sins of Marketing

1. The company is not sufficiently market focused and customer driven.
2. The company does not fully understand its target customers.
3. The company needs to better define and monitor its competitors.
4. The company has not properly managed its relationships with its stakeholders.
5. The company is not good at finding new opportunities.
6. The company's marketing plans and planning process are deficient.
7. The company's product and service policies need tightening.
8. The company's brand-building and communications skills are weak.
9. The company is not well organized to carry on effective and efficient marketing.
10. The company has not made maximum use of technology.

Notes

1. Doug Hall, *Jump Start Your Business Brain* (Cincinnati, OH: Brain Brew Books, 2001), p. 3.
2. Naomi Klein, *No Logo* (London: Flamingo, 2000).
3. There are over 136 books listed on Amazon.com with the words "Deadly Sins." A couple in the management literature include David L. Dotlich and Peter C. Cairo, *Why CEOs Fail: The 11 Deadly Sins and How NOT to Commit Them*, and Jonathan Ellis and Rene Tissen, *The Seven Deadly Sins of Management* (London: Profile Books, 2003).

Chapter 1

Your Company Is Not Sufficiently Market Focused and Customer Driven

Here we single out two sides of the most handicapping deficiency in most companies. We find either that your company has not gained insight into your market opportunities, or that your company is not well-organized to serve and deliver what your target customers want and expect.

INSUFFICIENT MARKET FOCUS

What indicates that your marketers have not sufficiently analyzed your market?

Signs:

- Poor identification of market segments.
- Insufficient prioritization of market segments.
- No market segment managers.

Poor Identification of Market Segments

We ask this question: "Who are you trying to sell to?" Please don't answer "Everyone." It's not acceptable.

I remember hearing this when I asked this question to top executives of the giant Sears chain store. "We sell to everyone. Everyone buys something at our store . . . clothing, hammers, appliances. . . ." Then I asked: "Do you get a lot of teenagers shopping for their clothes at Sears?" "No, not as many as we would like. But we do get their mothers shopping at Sears." "So not every group is a strong shopper at Sears." "Yes, we admit that." "Then why don't you focus on the groups that really like your merchandise and service, instead of trying to get everyone into your store?" He didn't have an answer.

Fortunately, most companies don't answer "Everyone." But this doesn't mean they are correctly focused. A women's dress shop might say: "We sell clothing to women between ages 20 and 50." I say, that's a pretty large group whose needs are quite varied. Younger women are more likely to dress for the social scene while the 35+ group is probably more interested in utility in clothes for work and home.

There's a story told about how Les Wexner started his successful Limited chain of women's stores. Les's father ran a women's store that carried all kinds of dresses for different ages. Les went to Ohio State where his marketing instructor spoke about segmentation. He asked his dad: "Why do we carry so many dresses for so many women?" His dad answered: "The answer is obvious: How would I know what woman will walk into the store? Les, I feel that I am wasting my money sending you to college." When Les took over the business, it was his turn to limit the merchandise, in this case to young women in their twenties and to the kind of clothes they like. And he did everything to focus on this group, including hiring young sales clerks of the same age, playing music in the store that young women liked, and using colors that appealed to this group. And he renamed the store the Limited.

Insufficient Prioritization of Market Segments

Many companies do identify different market segments and prepare offerings for each chosen segment. Thus an aluminum manufacturer may sell aluminum on different terms to airplane manufacturers, car manufacturers, construction contractors, and kitchen appliance manufacturers. My question is whether that company has really measured the relative attractiveness of each segment. Obviously the aluminum company is investing resources to serve each segment, but has it estimated the likely rates of return on its investment (ROI) in the different segments? Has it prioritized the segments and reallocated its resources to the more profitable segments?

No Market Segment Managers

The more important segments should have managers who are empowered to ask for budgets that they believe will produce the company's target rate of return. And they should be rewarded accordingly. But not that many companies have appointed clear leaders to manage the more important segments.

Solutions:

- Adopt more advanced techniques in segmentation, such as benefit segmentation, value segmentation, and loyalty segmentation.
- Prioritize the most important segments.
- Specialize the sales force.

Needed: Better Market Segmentation Techniques

Most companies can do a better job of segmenting their market than they are currently doing. Too many are stopping their segmentation at the demographic or descriptive level. A given demographic group, (say) 30- to 50-year-old men, usually contains quite different individuals with varying needs, preferences, and values. Ford found this out when it launched its new Mustang automobile to appeal to young sports-minded drivers, only to find that many young people were not so interested and many older people rushed to buy the car.

In business-to-business marketing, companies tend to segment buyers into large customers, medium-size customers, and small customers. But if I want to sell business software to small companies, I had better start distinguishing between the needs of small law firms, accounting firms, and medical firms, and probably focus on only one of these and become the supplier of choice.

In general, first try to segment the members of a market by different needs or sought benefits. Then try to find demographic descriptors that might correlate with these needs and benefits to make the search for these prospects easier.

Prioritize the Segments!

Suppose your company has identified more than one segment. For example, IBM sells mainframe computers to companies in numerous industries. That didn't stop IBM from recognizing that certain segments were much more important than others. IBM listed 12 industries in particular where they would focus their effort, industries such as banking, insurance, hotels, telecommunications, and transportation. By focusing their research on these industries they were able to design more compelling offerings than unfocused competitors could present.

"Verticalize" Your Sales Force

If the customer segments are quite different, then you should develop specialized sales forces. IBM learned long ago that sending an IBM salesperson in the morning to sell a computer system to a bank and in the afternoon to sell a computer system to a hotel chain didn't result in much business. The salesperson knew too little about the needs of banks or hotels. IBM found out that it is better to hire ex-bankers to sell to banks and ex-hoteliers to sell to hotels. They have deep experience in these respective industries, and probably a network of relationships, all of which puts them in a much better position to sell effectively.

DuPont also learned how important it is to organize by customer segments. In their fiber division, they used to have salespersons specialized by nylon, orlon, and dacron. A nylon salesperson was expected to know all the different industries that buy nylon, such as women's clothing manufacturers, furniture manufacturers, boat sales manufacturers, auto tire manufacturers, and so on. Finally DuPont reorganized and assigned salespeople to cover a particular customer market such as women's clothing, furniture, floor covering, boating, and so on. And they were to represent all the fibers, not just one, giving the customers what they want.

The message: Define your segments carefully, prioritize them, and assign customer segment managers to the most important segments.

INSUFFICIENT CUSTOMER ORIENTATION

What indicates that your company is not sufficiently organized to do an especially good job of serving and satisfying your customers? Here are the signs:

Signs:

- Most employees think that it is the job of marketing and sales to serve the customers.
- There is no training program to create a customer culture.
- There are no incentives to treat the customer especially well.

It's the Job of Marketing and Sales to Get, Serve, and Satisfy Customers!

Companies have found it convenient to organize their employees into departments designed to carry out specific responsibilities. A scientist will spend her time in the laboratory, not with customers; a production engineer will spend his time in the factory, not with customers; a purchasing person will spend her time with salespeople, not with customers; and accountants and finance people will spend their time enjoying numbers, not customers.

The result is that people working in these departments naturally assume that another department—sales and marketing—will handle customers. Yet we know that every department can damage customer relations. Customers get angry when the product is poorly made, when it is delivered late, and when the invoice is wrong, and the company loses its customers through no fault of marketing.

No Need to Train Others to Serve Customers

Training people in other departments to "think customers" is expensive. Courses have to be designed, teachers hired, and people have to take time away from their other, more pressing activities to hear about customers.

No Metrics, Incentives, or Sanctions Are in Place for Improving Customer Service

People know how they are measured by their departments and that's what counts. They will behave accordingly. In the absence of clear measures of the impact of their actions on customers, they will not pay much attention to customers on a day-to-day basis.

Solutions:

- Develop a clear hierarchy of company values with customers at the top.
- Engage in activities that will produce more "customer consciousness" in employees and the company's agents.
- Make it easy for customers to reach the company by phone, fax, or e-mail with inquiries, suggestions, and complaints and respond quickly.

Develop a Clear Hierarchy of Company Values with Customers at the Top

Ask senior management the following question: "What is the main group that you are working so hard to satisfy?" Many senior managers will quickly answer: "The stockholders. They own the company. They judge our performance. They affect our cost of capital. They take the risk. Their opinion of us shows up daily in the movement of our stock price. Our first obligation is to the stockholders and that's why we look at everything in terms of shareholder value."

I would challenge this on the grounds that making the stockholders paramount is the least helpful way to serve them. I would rather endorse Johnson & Johnson's ordering of groups: J&J declares that "Customers come first, employees come second, and this will give the investors the best results."

The Marriott Hotel chain puts the ordering slightly differently. "We first hire and train the best employees. If the employees are happy, they will serve the customers enthusiastically and competently. Then the customers will come back to our hotels. This will produce the most profits for the investors." Not surprisingly, Hal Rosenbluth, who heads one of the largest travel agencies, picks up the same theme in his book bearing the provocative title, *The Customer Comes Second.*[1]

The main point is clear: Companies must obsess about their customers and their employees because if they are not satisfied, the firm might as well close down.

Undertake Activities That Will Produce a Stronger "Customer Consciousness"

Shifting a company from one orientation to another is a formidable task. Companies develop deep cultures involving valuing certain things and not others. Thus an engineering-oriented company will focus on designing state-of-the-art products and on designing the best production systems as the key to winning the competitive battle. Engineers assume that most customers will be drawn to the best products and lowest costs. But this is a naïve view of customers, because customers will vary greatly in what they interpret as best products and appropriate prices and costs.

To change an ingrained culture to put customers at the center of the company universe would take strong and determined new leadership. Here we can only suggest some key steps to take:

- *Develop a clear hierarchy of groups and values.* We have already stressed the importance of establishing and disseminating a clear hierarchy of customer groups and values to company personnel.

- *Show how each employee's behavior can affect customers.* Show the employees in each department how their specific actions can positively or negatively affect the attraction or retention of customers. Spotlight specific cases of how customers have been either won or lost by departmental behavior. Show how each employee needs to be serving customers or serving someone in the company who is serving the customers.

- *Regularly feature findings on customer satisfaction.* Measure customer satisfaction overall, and by customer groups and by specific items (product, service, price, etc.). Report the scores to the various departments, with a view to inspiring everyone to seek to improve customer satisfaction each period. One action is to include a bonus if customer satisfaction rises or reaches a certain point. Include in every employee's paycheck envelope the statement that their check is being paid by the customers.

- *Sponsor a companywide training program in customer service and satisfaction.* The company can sponsor short classes designed for different departments to train the department's personnel in better customer service. The aim is to define the company's brand and values and to get the employees to "live the brand." Thus Wal-Mart's people are determined to provide goods at the lowest possible cost. Ritz-Carlton employees are determined to provide the best hospitality service. Volvo's people are determined to design the safest automobiles. In fact, Volvo resisted adding a global positioning system (GPS) in its new models because the screen poses a danger when the driver takes his eyes off the road. To live the brand, Volvo engineers resisted adding GPS, but finally designed a screen that was the easiest and safest to use.

- *Make sure that all the distributors and dealers also are customer obsessed.* It doesn't help a company if its people are customer-obsessed but its agents are not. The company must move its partners into the same mindset if a customer orientation is to bear fruit.

Make It Easy for Customers to Reach the Company

I am continually frustrated when phoning a leading electronics retailer and listening to a two-minute message and finding it next to impossible to reach a live person. And when I reach a live person and ask if the store is carrying a certain product, she says that she will check and then I hold the phone for another three minutes, only to learn that they are out of stock. And this store runs ads on how friendly they are!

Your company needs to make it super-easy for customers to reach you by phone, fax, mail, or e-mail. Furthermore, you should set a high standard for answering quickly. Amazon says that mail and e-mail must be answered within two days and telephone calls within four rings. The cost of this level of service is small in comparison with the cost of losing customers.

Note

1. Hal Rosenbluth and Diane McFerrin Peters, *The Customer Comes Second: Put Your People First and Watch 'Em Kick Butt* (New York: HarperBusiness, 2002).

Chapter 2

Your Company Does Not Fully Understand Its Target Customers

Signs:

- Your last study of customers was done three years ago.
- Customers are not buying your product at the expected rate; competitor's products are selling better.
- There is a high level of customer returns and complaints.

WEAK INFORMATION ON TARGET CUSTOMERS

The first question I ask is "Who is your target customer?" If the answer is not clear, then the first task is to dialog on this question.

If the answer is clear, I ask for a copy of the latest market research study describing how the company's target customers think, act, and feel. The worst response is, "We don't have such a study." The next-worst response is: "Here it is," and you are handed a three-year-old hardcover-bound study. What's worse, it has never been opened or used. Today's customers cannot possibly think, act, and feel as they did three years ago. It was prosperity then; today it might be recession. We can even raise questions about whether the study methodology was the best way to achieve insight into the target customers.

The challenge is even more daunting: How can your company listen continuously to the "voice of the customer"? The best answer is to engage in continuous dialogue with customers in their offices, in the stores, over the phone, and through e-mail. In this way the company learns and can customize appropriate offerings, services, and messages for different customers.[1]

SALES ARE LAGGING BEHIND EXPECTATIONS

A company's marketing plan sets sales, cost, and profit goals for the year, broken into quarterly or monthly expectations. When performance is disappointing, causes must be assigned. Is the fault poor economic conditions, an unfavorable shift in customer preferences, a superior competitive offering, or the wrong pricing? How should the company revise its strategy and offerings?

HIGH LEVEL OF CUSTOMER RETURNS AND COMPLAINTS

A clear sign of a company not understanding its customers is when it receives a lot of returned merchandise and complaints. Product returns result from a company misrepresenting or poorly communicating its offerings. Catalog marketers suffer when they don't clearly define the features of a product and it is returned.

Customer complaints can arise from a wide range of irritations. The customer finds it hard to get information; the invoice is inaccurate; the employee is rude or incompetent. Complaints don't risk losing one customer; every complainer might tell ten acquaintances who in turn further spread negative news about the company. Clearly a company must respond quickly and appropriately to complaining customers. Some studies document the surprising result that customers who have complained and who have received a quick resolution often end up being more loyal to the company than customers who never complained![2]

Solutions:

- Do more sophisticated consumer research.
- Use more analytical techniques.
- Establish customer and dealer panels.
- Install customer relationship marketing software and do data mining.

NEEDED: MORE AND BETTER CUSTOMER RESEARCH

The current buzzword is *customer insight*. The company that gains deeper insight into customers' needs, perceptions, preferences, and behavior will gain the competitive edge. What research does your company undertake to gain customer insight? Sometimes the best research consists of continuously dialoging with your target consumers, singly and in groups. One can pick up many ideas and insights in this way. However, street talk, while valuable, is not sufficient. More formal approaches are needed that would include:

- Focus groups.
- Surveys.
- Depth interviewing.
- In-home research.
- In-store research.
- Mystery shopping.

Focus Groups

One can learn a great deal by inviting 8 to 12 individuals to participate in a discussion led by a skilled moderator on a focused topic, such as a new product idea, an existing product, a new communication approach, or some other marketing issue. The moderator's task is to ask questions, solicit comments, and manage the discussion in a way that maintains interest, moves it forward, and brings out everyone's views.

I observed a focus group sponsored by Mercedes to test U.S. consumers' interest in Mercedes' new Smart Car, a diminutive but stylish car that is a hit in Europe. But the participants were largely skeptical, saying that the car looked unsafe, was too expensive, and perhaps might be considered only if they needed a third car for short shopping trips. After hearing this from several focus groups, Mercedes decided not to introduce the car in the United States.

The use of one or more focus groups will most likely yield some insights into consumer needs, views, attitudes, and likely behavior. The research is exploratory in that without a follow-up statistical survey, there is no way to tell how representative the findings are.

Surveys

Designing a survey is the answer to this problem. The researcher draws up a careful questionnaire that is sent to and answered by a representative sample of the target population. This will give a reliable picture of the attitudes of the population from which the sample is drawn, providing that all the interviewees answer the questions. When there are a lot of noncooperating respondents, the hope is that the noncooperators do not differ significantly from the cooperators.

Depth Interviewing

Even if every respondent faithfully answers the questionnaire, this is not likely to provide a deep insight into consumer motivations. People may withhold, rationalize, or not be in touch with their true feelings. This has given rise to one-to-one in-depth interviews based on Freudian, Jungian, or other psychological approaches that may include projective techniques that bypass their rational faculties. But like focus groups, it is difficult to know how representative the findings are relative to the general population.

In-Home Research

More behavior-oriented researchers prefer to observe people's behavior in real situations than to ask them questions. This has given rise to increased in-home research where families agree to carry on their normal activities (cooking, eating, and so on) while researchers armed with a video camera record their interactions and talk. Researchers hope to gain insights into how people handle cooking or eating situations or make clothing choices, for example.

In-Store Research

Besides observing behavior in the home, some researchers are now actively studying the behavior of shoppers in stores. Paco Underhill wrote up his findings in his book, *Why We Buy: The Science of Shopping.*[3] The book offers the following advice for designing the retail space in order to keep shoppers spending:

- *Honor the "transition zone."* Upon entering a store, shoppers will likely be moving too fast to respond positively to signs, merchandise, or sales clerks. They will start slowing down in the transition zone and begin noticing things.
- *Make merchandise available to the touch.* A store can offer the finest, cheapest, sexiest goods, but if the shopper can't handle or try them, much of their appeal can be lost.
- *Men don't ask questions.* Men usually move faster than women through the store's aisles. It's hard to get them to look at anything they hadn't intended to buy. Also—men generally don't like asking where things are. They would rather leave the store than ask a clerk.

Mystery Shopping

A third behavior-oriented research approach is to hire people to act as shoppers and report on the behavior of clerks in company and competitor locations. Thus a bank could hire mystery shoppers to open accounts and report back on their experience. Companies will often be surprised at the failure of their own employees to treat customers in the right way.

I remember acting as a customer in a Pizza Inn prior to giving a talk to their management. I was appalled by how long it took for the staff to take my order, how slow the staff was in bringing it to the table, and how bad the pizza tasted. I reported this to senior management and they took immediate steps to correct the situation.

USE MORE ANALYTICAL TECHNIQUES

Beyond collecting raw data, companies need to employ more sophisticated tools for assessing consumer behavior. Here are some examples.

Consumer Needs

Consumer needs could be probed more deeply by psychological in-depth interviewing consisting of projective techniques such as word associations, sentence completions, and thematic apperception tests (TATs). Beyond this, some researchers use a laddering technique in which they follow the consumer's explanation with another probing question. For example, the consumer may say that she bought a Mercedes because it is better engineered. "Why is this important to you?" "Because the car will ride more smoothly." "Why is this important to you?" "Because I like to be comfortable." "Why is this important to you?" "Because I feel important and deserve the best." Thus we move from a simple explanation to a much deeper set of meanings motivating the customer.

Consumer Perceptions

Using a technique called *perceptual mapping*, the researcher can show how consumers perceive different brands in relation to a set of attributes. Suppose consumers are asked to rate car brands on two dimensions, status and reliability. The research might show that the average consumer would position Jaguar as high in status but medium in reliability and rate Toyota as medium in status and high in reliability. By viewing all the cars in the perceptual mapping space, one can conclude which cars are the closest competitors to any particular brand.

Consumer Preferences

Companies can use a number of techniques to assess consumer preferences. Among the simpler approaches are consumer ratings and rankings. A more sophisticated approach is *conjoint analysis*, where consumers rank their choices among a hypothetical set of fully described concepts. Their choices can be analyzed to reveal the relative importance consumers place on each attribute, which guides the company to know which concept would be the most successful.

Consumer data also can be analyzed by regression, discriminant, and cluster analysis methods to lead to predictions of how likely consumers are to respond to different stimuli (price, features, appeals, and so on). *Predictive analytics* are used by direct mailers to select the prospects who have the highest probability of responding positively to an offer.

Ethnographic Research

Much consumer behavior is conditioned by the beliefs, norms, and values held by a specific social group, whether they are upper-class teenagers, Polish-American seniors, or Mormon believers in Utah. The tools of social anthropology promise to shed light on many aspects of behavior that are not as readily visible through ordinary survey research.

ESTABLISH CUSTOMER AND DEALER PANELS

Your company can benefit by recruiting a set of your customers who agree to be periodically interviewed about new ideas, products, and communications. The panel members can be reached by mail, fax, e-mail, or phone. You can reward the panel members with money or goods. The panel represents a built-in focus group that is chosen to represent the target population. You should also run dealer and supplier panels to stay in touch with their views.

Your company could go further and set up an online chat room where your customers and prospects can exchange views. This would have the most value with companies whose customers are great fans—companies such as Harley Davidson or Apple Computer. These fans will exchange information, arrange meetings, and further build a strong community. Your company will gather insight by monitoring the conversations. But the company whose customers are less sanguine should not sponsor a chat room. Bad opinions of the company would spread faster. At best, such a company should audit conversations in regular chat rooms to catch any negative talk that calls for quick remedies.

INSTALL CUSTOMER RELATIONSHIP MANAGEMENT (CRM) SOFTWARE AND PERFORM DATA MINING

Companies are increasingly gathering information about a customer's past purchases, demographics, and psychographics in the hope of gaining a finer understanding of each customer. Of these strands of information, past purchases serve as the most useful information, indicating the customer's revealed preferences. The past purchases of one customer may reveal him to be an early buyer of new electronics products, making the customer a good target for the company's next new electronics product. Such customer data are stored in a *data warehouse*. A sample of these data is put into a *data mart* and analyzed by skilled *data miners*. The data miners are often able to spot new *segments* that can represent a new opportunity for the company. Or they can spot *trends* in products, features, or services that might alert them to new offerings. They can also test the effectiveness of predictive analytics in reaching the best prospects.

Notes

1. Quote Don Peppers and Martha Rogers, *The One-to-One Future* (New York: Doubleday/Currency, 1993).
2. TAIC studies.
3. Paco Underhill, *Why We Buy: The Science of Shopping* (New York: Simon & Schuster, 1999).

Chapter 3

Your Company Needs to Better Define and Monitor Its Competitors

Signs:

- Your company overfocuses on its near competitors and misses distant competitors and disruptive technologies.
- Your company lacks a system for gathering and distributing competitive intelligence.

YOU ARE OVERFOCUSING ON THE WRONG COMPETITOR

Companies normally find it easy to name their competitors.

- McDonald's would name Burger King and Wendy's. If they thought more broadly, they would include Taco Bell, Pizza Hut, and Subway. And to broaden it further, they should include supermarkets that have added prepared foods.
- U.S. Steel would name Bethlehem Steel and other integrated steel companies, and maybe even companies like Nucor (nonintegrated steel manufacturer). But the real question is whether U.S. Steel is paying enough attention to the inroads being made by the aluminum and plastic industries. For example, auto makers are

choosing to replace a lot of steel in their cars with plastic materials. Who would ever think that General Electric's Plastics Division competed with U.S. Steel?

YOU DON'T HAVE A SYSTEM FOR ORGANIZING COMPETITIVE INTELLIGENCE

How much information does a typical company have about its competitors? If Xerox is bidding against Sharp for a large contract involving 1,000 copiers, how much does Xerox know about the bidding practices of Sharp? Who in Xerox keeps information on each competitor's objectives, resources, strategies, and practices? Is this in the hands of a *competitive intelligence* office, or does the Xerox salesperson have to hunt for some other colleagues who have had previous experience competing against Sharp?

Solutions:

- Establish a person or office for competitive intelligence.
- Hire away people from competitors.
- Watch every new technology that might hurt the company.
- Prepare offerings similar to your competitors'.

ESTABLISH A PERSON OR OFFICE FOR COMPETITIVE INTELLIGENCE

A company would be wise to establish a person or office responsible for *collecting* and *disseminating* competitive intelligence. Think of this as setting up a librarian who is gifted at tracking news about competitors on the Internet and developing competitor profiles. Any company employee facing a competitor could contact this person and be briefed on how the competitor thinks and reacts.

HIRE AWAY PEOPLE FROM COMPETITORS

Your company should consider hiring people away from your major competitors. This should not be done to steal secrets that belong to the other companies (this is unlawful and you will be sued) but to get to know how the competitor thinks and acts.

I remember when IBM hired away a young manager from Sun Microsystems and after a few years asked him to appear before the IBM Board of Directors and pretend to be Scott McNealy, CEO of Sun, and tell what he is planning to do to IBM. The young former Sun employee looked directly at the 13 members of the IBM Board and avowed:

> *My company, Sun Microsystems, will bury you! We are going to succeed because you, IBM, think that the*

future lies in boxes (mainframes) but we think the future lies in building networks to connect these boxes. The boxes will become commodities but building networks will remain a highly specialized skill carrying good margins.

IBM's Board was startled by his directness but dismissed his message. Shortly thereafter IBM entered a long period of decline and it wasn't until some years later when their new president, Lou Gerstner, acclaimed IBM to be a "network-centric company." Had IBM heeded the young man's message earlier, its fortunes would not have dimmed that much.

MONITOR EVERY NEW TECHNOLOGY

A greater threat to many companies is not an existing competitor so much as a new and better technology. Professor Clayton Christensen of Harvard calls this a disruptive technology.[1] Many examples can be cited. The mechanical adding machine made the abacus obsolete and the electronic calculator made the slide rule obsolete. The automobile replaced the horse-and-buggy carriage. Some types of surgeries were made obsolete by the invention of a pill.

Your company must monitor every technology that may threaten to displace its basic offering or production process. Even better, you should view these threatening technologies as investment options. By betting some money on these new technologies, the company may protect its future. Our maxim: "Every company should cannibalize itself before someone else does."

The story is told about the General Electric manager of the vacuum tube division who came into his boss's office boasting of having increased the vacuum tube business by 20 percent. His boss fired him. "You increased the vacuum business because our competitors went out of business. That was easy. What you should have done is got us into the transistor business. You kept us in the past when you should have prepared us for the future!"

PREPARE OFFERINGS SIMILAR TO THOSE OF YOUR COMPETITORS

Your company may enjoy a well-recognized price-point position in the market. Thus Marriott originally positioned itself as an upper mid-level hotel chain. But what would happen if a growing number of businesspeople seek less expensive accommodations? This possibility led Marriott to design a motel system called Courtyard for business travelers who didn't want an expensive hotel with a fancy restaurant and large convention facilities. And Courtyard was a runaway success. Then Marriott recognized the need for a still less expensive motel system for traveling families and built Fairfield Inn, another successful motel system. Subsequently Marriott introduced other hotel concepts, such as Residence Inns, Marriott Suites, Marriott Resorts, and others. This meant that Marriott would not be vulnerable to a single positioning concept but would be safe with properties positioned in several hospitality classes.

A similar story can be told about the Austrian firm Swarovski, maker of fine crystals. One of its divisions makes fine lead crystals for mountings on chandelier frames. Their crystals are the finest and cost the most. Subsequently a European competitor emerged who charged 20 percent less than Swarovski, and then an Egyptian competitor emerged who charged 50 percent less! What should Swarovski do? The easy way out is that Swarovski should lower its price, but this would cut into its profits greatly. A better answer is to use strong pull branding to get hotels and homes that buy chandeliers to insist on Swarovski crystal. A still better answer is to show chandelier makers or hotels how they can save money or time using Swarovski crystal because they don't have to be cleaned as often or they can be mounted quickly with a special Swarovski patented process. Maybe the best answer is for Swarovski to buy the European competitor and the Egyptian competitor or to start lower-end businesses so that the crystal buyer can buy "good, better, or best" crystal depending on her budget. Again, "If you are going to be cannibalized, be the first to cannibalize yourself."

A company should recognize that there are several value/price positionings available in any market. They are:

- Less for much less (Southwest Airlines).
- The same for less (Wal-Mart).
- The same for the same (Tide).
- The same for more money (not recommended).
- More for the same (Lexus).
- More for more (Mercedes, Haagen-Dazs).

I am not recommending that a company make an offering at all six levels. Sears had it right when they offered radios at three levels: "good, better, and best."

Note

1. Clayton M. Christensen, *The Innovator's Dilemma: When New Technologies Cause Great Firms to Fail* (Boston: Harvard Business School Press, 1997).

Chapter 4

Your Company Has Not Properly Managed Its Relationships with Its Stakeholders

Signs:

- Your employees are not happy.
- You have not attracted the best suppliers.
- You don't have the best distributors and your dealers are unhappy.
- Your investors are not happy.

YOUR EMPLOYEES ARE NOT HAPPY

Tom Peters, management guru and co-author of *In Search of Excellence*, would claim that he could enter a company and tell within 15 minutes whether the employees were happy or disgruntled. A disgruntled employee can sabotage a company. Signs of unhappy employees would include high employee turnover, frequent failure to carry out policies, strong factionalism, and negative views of other company departments.

YOU HAVE SECOND-RATE SUPPLIERS

Suppliers differ greatly in their capacities to deliver quality products and services. Companies claiming high-quality goods need high-quality suppliers. But high-quality suppliers may already be producing at capacity and not be able to take on another customer. Or they may be limited to serving only one competitor in each industry. Your company would have to hire the second-best supplier and this may handicap its claim to have the highest quality.

Your company may choose to work with second-rate suppliers to bring down purchase costs. But you will probably incur other and higher costs in dealing with a second-rate supplier.

YOUR DISTRIBUTORS LEAVE A LOT TO BE DESIRED

Your company hires distributors and dealers because they can reach your target customers better than you can do on your own. You expect them to give priority attention to your products even when they carry competitors' products. But you must make your terms rewarding to your distributors. They must feel that they gain as much or more selling your company's products as selling the other products they carry.

YOUR INVESTORS ARE NOT SATISFIED

Investor satisfaction is quickly revealed by how long investors keep their funds invested in your company's stock. A bad sign is a falling share price or higher loan interest rates. This raises your cost of capital and therefore your cost of business, all pointing to lower profits in the future.

Solutions:

- Move from zero-sum thinking to positive-sum thinking.
- Manage employees better.
- Manage supplier relations better.
- Manage distributors and dealers better.
- Manage investors better.

MOVE TO POSITIVE-SUM THINKING

In earlier times, a businessperson thought that the size of the pie was fixed. His conclusion: He could gain the most by paying his partners—employees, suppliers, distributors—the least. This is zero-sum thinking. Today, there is growing evidence that your economic results will vary with the manner in which you treat your partners. Fred Reichheld, in his *Loyalty Rules!*, describes many successful companies that reward their employees, suppliers, and distributors generously, and this creates a larger pie, including the share that goes to your company.[1] Your company will attract better and more motivated employees, suppliers, and distributors, and they will manage as a team to outperform the competitors.

MANAGE EMPLOYEES BETTER

Employees work best when they are well chosen, well trained, well motivated, and well respected. This doesn't happen in a firm that just hires loads of people, gives them little or no training, gives them little latitude in decision making, and frequently criticizes their work. Such workers can easily become in-company saboteurs.

Employees should not be hired until senior management has clearly defined the company's values, vision, mission, positioning, and target customers. Then the company can search for the right people, train them appropriately, empower them, and know they will "live the company's brand."

Enlightened companies even change the language—not *employees* but *associates* or *partners*. At Southwest Airlines, CEO Herb Kelleher renamed the Human Resources Department the People Department.

It is a new paradigm for companies to see their employees as creative and responsible, especially when they are given a measure of respect. Smart companies adopt an *internal marketing* perspective in that they see their employees as differing in their needs, and by knowing their individual needs, the company can better serve and satisfy them. I remember a hospital that had a high rate of nurse turnover, all because it insisted on the same hours for all nurses, regardless of whether they were single, married, or with children. Only when a new nurse administrator took over and established flexible working hours and better working conditions did the hospital start attracting and retaining a competent and satisfied nursing staff.

MANAGE SUPPLIER RELATIONS BETTER

Given that suppliers vary in quality and performance, a company should seek the best suppliers and reward them at a level that will bring forth their best efforts. Companies are continually reducing the number of their suppliers. The old game—using three suppliers in a category, giving 60 percent to the lead supplier, 30 percent to a second supplier, and 10 percent to a third supplier—in order to keep them all on edge and competing for the company's business—is giving way to choosing one excellent supplier in each category. The auto industry has moved in this direction, contracting with one firm to supply the seating, another the braking system, and another the air conditioning system. The company and its supplier partners co-invest in each other and act as a winning team in designing and making cars. This level of partnership can increase the company's quality, productivity, and innovativeness while reducing costs.

MANAGE DISTRIBUTORS AND DEALERS BETTER

Your company needs to identify and attract the best distributors (wholesalers, dealers, agents, and retailers). Their quality makes a great difference in your ability to reach and satisfy the end users. The key is to get the distributors to place a high value on their relationship with you and to put out special effort on your behalf. Much depends on the terms of engagement you set with your distributors.

Caterpillar, the world's leading earthmoving equipment company, has a stellar relationship with its dealers:

> *Local dealers who are long-established members of their communities can get closer to customers than a global company can on its own; but to tap the full potential of such dealers, a company must forge extremely close ties with them and integrate them into its critical business systems. When treated in this way, dealers can serve as sources of market information and intelligence, as proxies for customers, as consultants, and as problem solvers. Indeed, our dealers play a vital role in almost*

> *every aspect of our business, including product design and delivery, service and field support and the management of replacement-part inventories. Dealers can be much more than a channel to customers.*[2]

Caterpillar's senior management see their dealers as their major competitive advantage and would avoid doing anything that might damage the sense of partnership.

Besides hiring the best distributors, a company must maintain a continuous learning relationship. Companies should especially set up extranets with their distributors that can serve several purposes, including informing the distributors of new ideas and developments and facilitating the ordering, delivery, and payment cycle.

Notes

1. Frederick F. Reichheld, *Loyalty Rules! How Today's Leaders Build Lasting Relationships* (Boston: Harvard Business School Press, 2001).
2. Statement about Caterpillar.

Chapter 5

Your Company Is Not Good at Finding New Opportunities

Signs:

- Your company has not identified any exciting new opportunities in recent years.
- The new ideas that your company has launched have largely failed.

YOUR COMPANY HAS NOT DONE WELL IN FINDING NEW OPPORTUNITIES

An interesting question for your company is "How many new products and services did you launch in the last five years?" Companies will give different answers to this. The 3M Company would cite many new products. In fact, the company makes a point of wanting to derive 30 percent of its current revenue from products introduced in the last five years.

On the other hand, major companies such as Coca-Cola and Procter & Gamble (P&G) give a less rosy answer. In the case of Coca-Cola, the most successful new beverages—fruit juices, energy beverages, bottled water—were introduced by competitors first. At best, Coca-Cola followed them and in some cases grew by acquiring them.

The great P&G cannot boast of introducing many successful new products in the last five years through their own R&D efforts. To compensate, P&G has gone on an acquisition binge, growing by buying companies in cosmetics, toiletries, and food.

The lack of company innovation points either to a company that fails to systematically find and research new opportunities or to one that invests in many new opportunities but with disappointing results.

MOST OF YOUR INITIATIVES HAVE FAILED

Good opportunities can be ruined by poor new product management processes. Somehow the company either lets poor opportunities go through or botches up good opportunities at some stage such as concept development, concept testing, prototype development, prototype testing, business and marketing planning, test marketing, or product launch.

Solutions:

- Set up a system for stimulating the flow of new ideas from your partners.
- Utilize creativity systems for generating new ideas.

SET UP A SYSTEM FOR STIMULATING IDEAS FROM YOUR PARTNERS

Some companies believe there are no new opportunities. They say their industry is mature. Or they say that they are selling a commodity. But there is no such thing as a mature market or a commodity. It's only that your beliefs are getting in the way of your imagination. Starbucks didn't see the coffee market as mature.

No company has to go without new ideas. First of all, the company's employees probably have many ideas for improvement. All they lack is knowing where to send these ideas and the motivation to send them. Second, the company's suppliers, distributors, advertising agency, and other partners probably could suggest many new ideas. Third, there are systematic ways to help employees generate new ideas.

In an excellent article called "Bringing Silicon Valley Inside Your Company," Gary Hamel presented one recipe for generating successful new ideas.[1] Silicon Valley, he said, scored its successes because it was the site of three markets: an *idea market*, a *capital market*, and a *talent market*. Many creative and entrepreneurial people poured into the Valley with new ideas, especially for starting dot.coms. Venture-capital firms abounded to lend money to people with superior ideas. And the Valley attracted many talented people who could write software and implement ideas.

The implication is that companies need to duplicate Silicon Valley internally. The company should place a high value on new ideas and facilitate their collection and evaluation. The better ideas would draw on an internal pool of money to facilitate research and development.

The best ideas would then be assigned to the right talent to develop and launch them.

To manage the idea flow, the company should appoint a high-level executive to be the Idea Captain. He or she should have an Idea Committee with representation from each major department. Everyone in the company as well as in the partner companies should know the name, address, and e-mail of this committee and should be encouraged to send ideas to this committee. The Idea Committee should meet every few weeks to review and evaluate the ideas, putting them into three piles, from poor, to good, to great-sounding ideas. The great-sounding ideas are assigned to different committee members to report back. If the report is positive, then some money would be granted for further research and development. Those ideas that continue to look strong will be pushed through further stage gates until they are either dropped or launched.

Everyone submitting an idea will be told of its fate. This would counter the belief that the committee isn't interested in ideas. The strongest ideas that are eventually implemented successfully should carry recognition to the proposers with either money, vacations, or other tangible rewards. Kodak, for example, pays $10,000 each year to its employees who have contributed top money-making or money-saving ideas. Another company gives back 10 percent of the savings or incremental profit to the proposing party or group.

USE CREATIVITY SYSTEMS FOR GENERATING NEW IDEAS

Many of the best ideas will come from observing major shifts in the market environment. The market environment consists of PESTE elements—Political, Economic, Social, Technological, and Environmental. Here are ideas that have emerged from observing trends in each component:

- *Political:* A company observes the difficulty of conducting accurate elections with paper ballots and invents a foolproof electronic voting machine.
- *Economic:* A company notes the high price of hotel rooms in Tokyo and invents a hotel that rents berths, not rooms, at a low price.
- *Social:* A company notices the difficulty of singles meeting new people and invents a dating service on the Internet.
- *Technological:* A company invents an electronic tablet for managers to write in long-hand instead of using a keyboard, and their notes are digitalized.
- *Environmental:* A company fights the high cost of energy by building windmills to generate electricity.

Companies can also use group or individual creativity techniques to stimulate new ideas. Group techniques include brainstorming, synectics, and several other techniques.[2]

Most companies search for new ideas by starting with their current product and varying it in some way. For example, a cereal company will think of adding raisins or nuts or more sugar or less sugar, or moving to wheat, or oats, or barley, or changing the package size or the brand name, and so on. This results in line extensions or brand extensions added to the cereal aisle in the supermarket. Their competitors do the same. The cereal aisle gets longer but not more profitable. Each product variant draws a smaller number of customers who defect from the larger-selling brands, with the result that the new products earn little and the old products earn less.

We call this *vertical marketing* and the techniques are numerous:

- Modulation
    - The *juice* manufacturer varies the sugar content, fruit concentrate, with or without vitamins . . .
- Sizing
    - *Potato chips* are offered in sizes 35 grams, 50 grams, 75 grams, 125 grams, 200 grams, multipacks . . .
- Packaging
    - *Nestle's Red Box chocolates* come in different containers: cheap paper box for the grocery trade, premium metal box for the gift trade . . .

- Design
  - *BMW* designs cars with different styling and features . . .
- Complements
  - *Biscuits* with sugar spread on them, with cinnamon, with chocolate, with white chocolate, with dark chocolate, filled biscuits . . .
- Efforts reduction
  - *Charles Schwab* offers different channels for transactions such as retail stores, telephone, Internet . . .

The main problem with vertical marketing is that this leads to a hyperfragmented market where few products have the volume to earn a lot of money.

Companies need to make use of an alternative idea-generating process that we call *lateral marketing.*[3] Lateral marketing is to think of your product in relation to another product, service, or idea. You are thinking *across two* products rather than *down one* product. For example, the cereal company could think of cereals + a snack. Instead of putting loose cereal in a box, they use the cereal in the form of a snack bar that can be carried and eaten any time. They may call this a health bar. Suddenly people are able to consume cereal any time of the day in a convenient form.

Here are other marketing breakthroughs arising from lateral thinking:

Gas station + food store = convenience store

Café + computers = cybercafe

Candy + toy = Kinder Surprise

Doll + teenager = Barbie Doll

Audio + portability = Walkman

Donation + adoption = "Be the godfather of a kid"

Flower + lives forever = artificial flowers

The lateral marketing concept has great potential to create new product categories, new markets, or new marketing mixes. These are badly needed because of the limitations of continuously varying the same product. In truth, a company needs to master both processes, vertical and lateral marketing, if it is to be successful at innovating.

Notes

1. Gary Hamel, "Bringing Slicon Valley Inside Your Company," *Harvard Business Review*, September–October 1999, pp. 71–84.
2. See, for example, James M. Higgins, *101 Creative Problem Solving Techniques* (Winter Park, FL: New Management Publishing Company, 1994).
3. Philip Kotler and Fernando Trias de Bes, *Lateral Marketing: A New Approach to Finding Breakthrough Ideas* (Hoboken, NJ: John Wiley & Sons, 2003).

Chapter 6

Your Company's Marketing Planning Process Is Deficient

Signs:

- Your marketing plan format does not carry the right components or logic.
- Your plans lack a means for simulating the financial implications of alternative strategies.
- Your plans lack contingency planning.

YOUR MARKETING PLAN IS MISSING CERTAIN COMPONENTS OR LOGIC

One has only to ask a company for some recent marketing plans to learn how weak marketing planning is. Marketing plans typically feature many numbers, budgets, and ads. But one looks in vain for a clear and compelling statement of objectives, strategy, and tactics. Even if the objectives are clear, there may be no compelling strategy. The tactics may be described but they may be totally unrelated to the strategy.

Ask the company for last year's plan and this year's plan for the same product. My bet is that the strategy and the tactics are the same in both cases. Namely, the latest plan is approximately the same as the previous plan. There is no new thinking. The planner has played safe by going with the older plan. He or she has ignored the new conditions in the market and the fact that a new strategy is called for and that different marketing instruments have changed in their effectiveness.

YOUR PLAN DOES NOT ALLOW FINANCIAL SIMULATION

The planning software may not permit simulating the impact of alternative strategies. It is not enough to describe (say) two strategies and estimate the sales and profits results from each. The plan needs to incorporate sales-response functions and cost functions that estimate the results of any combination of changes in product features, price, advertising, sales promotion, and sales force size.

YOUR PLAN DOES NOT CONSIDER CONTINGENCIES

Every plan is based on a set of assumptions about the market environment, competitive behavior, and costs. Does your plan visualize some alternative scenarios and state what your response would be? If the economy suddenly dips into a recession, have you figured out in advance what changes you would make in the plan?

Solutions:

- Establish a standard plan format including situational analysis, SWOT, major issues, objectives, strategy, tactics, budgets, and controls.
- Ask marketers what changes they would make if they were given 20 percent more budget or 20 percent less budget.
- Run an annual marketing awards program with prizes going to the best plans and performance.

ESTABLISH A CLEAR SEQUENCE OF PLAN COMPONENTS

A marketing plan should string together the following components: situational analysis; SWOT (strengths, weaknesses, opportunities, threats); major issues; objectives; strategy; tactics; budgets; and controls. Make sure that each stage follows from the previous stage. The situational analysis leads to sorting out the company's major strengths, weaknesses, opportunities, and threats. This leads to setting the right objectives. A strategy is formulated that promises to achieve the objectives. Tactics are developed that flesh out the strategy. The tactics have costs that add up to the budget request. Controls are put in place to check on whether the plan is delivering the objectives or whether changes are needed in mid-course.

ASK MANAGERS TO PREPARE FLEXIBLE BUDGETS

Senior management normally set *stretch goals* for the managers (e.g., "Grow your business by 10 percent this year"). It's not surprising, then, that the manager asks for a 10 percent increase in her budget. But senior management might say no and direct their managers to increase their sales by 10 percent without any increase in their budgets.

A better system would be *flexible budgeting*. Senior management should ask their managers what they think they can accomplish with (say) 20 percent more money. The managers would each have to describe how they would use the extra money and how much they think it would increase their sales and profits. Clearly those managers who claim that they can produce more than a 20 percent increase in their sales and profits should receive 20 percent more budget, if their case is credible.

Senior management should ask the same managers to estimate what would happen to their sales if the company was forced to reduce their budget by 20 percent.

Some managers will cry panic, that their sales will collapse drastically. Others would suggest a modest decline in sales.

Now this information can be used to reallocate the company's money to those who think they can do the most with extra funding. And the budget should be pared down less for those managers who think that budget cuts would hurt their sales the most.

The workability of flexible budgeting depends on the credibility of the estimates supplied by individual managers. Initially, managers may exaggerate what they could achieve with a larger budget or lose with a smaller budget. But they will be accountable for the results. After repeated use of this system, it will become clear which managers can competently forecast results and which ones are not to be trusted.

CELEBRATE THE BEST PLANS AT THE END OF THE YEAR

Each company department should celebrate its heroes who exemplify the best thinking in their area of competence. Each year the marketing department should celebrate the groups that developed the best marketing plans, judged by first-rate thinking and greatest success in the marketplace. Companies such as Becton-Dickenson, DuPont, and others honor their winning marketing plan teams each year. Not only do the teams feel proud and receive extra vacation or money, but the winning plans also are distributed to the other marketing managers to set higher standards for marketing planning and marketing implementation.

Chapter 7

Your Company's Product and Service Policies Need Tightening

Signs:

- The company has too many products and many are losing money.
- The company is giving away too many services free.
- The company is poor at cross-selling their products and services.

TOO MANY PRODUCTS THAT ARE NOT MAKING MONEY

Large companies are discovering that a small percentage of their products account for a large share of their profits. The problem starts from the fact that it is relatively easy to start new brands or line and brand extensions. Companies can launch products by creating different package sizes, ingredients, or flavors, all in the name of gaining more shelf space or satisfying more variable tastes of consumers. Companies add products more readily than they remove them. The product mix grows to contain too many losers. The company finally wakes up and in desperation axes a whole set of products to thin its product line and increase its profitability. But the product proliferation forces eventually resume again.

TOO MANY SERVICES ARE GIVEN AWAY FREE

Companies have traditionally thought less about their services surrounding a product than the products themselves. To win orders, salespeople will promise a lot of services: free delivery, free installation, free training. This happens even though these services carry a cost. Services that are given away free create two problems. First, customers tend to devalue them even if they take these services. Second, some services could have supplied a separate revenue stream that is lost when they are given away free. The challenge is to decide which services should be free and which ones should be priced and by how much.

TOO LITTLE CROSS-SELLING

Companies that sell a range of products and services often do a poor job of selling the other items beyond the one requested by the customer. Thus a buyer may buy a car from the dealer and then go elsewhere to buy insurance and get a loan. The customer who buys a suit may not be directed by the salesperson to shirts, ties, and shoes that might enhance the suit. The customer that takes out a checking account may not be told about the bank's other financial products, such as a savings account, or a college or home loan.

Solutions:

- The company needs to establish a system for tracking weak products and fixing or eliminating them.
- The company should offer and price services at different levels.
- The company should improve its processes for cross-selling and upselling.

ESTABLISH A PRODUCT TRACKING AND EVALUATION SYSTEM

Many years ago I proposed a product tracking and evaluation system that a company could use to distinguish its strong products from its weaker ones and make appropriate pruning decisions.[1] Today's companies need a system like this more than ever, given the explosion of product variants and the fact that many of them lose money for companies.

In 1999, Unilever found that 50 of its 1,600 brands, or 3 percent, accounted for 63 percent of its revenue.[2] Unilever proceeded to identify 400 of its strongest brands, calling them core or power brands. These were its current big money makers that had the potential to pull in much more sales and profits if they received more funding. They were brands—such as Knorr, Dove, Lipton, Hellman's—that could support more line, brand, channel, and geographical extension. The other 1,200 brands would be reduced in number through sale, liquidation, or combination. Ultimately Unilever would sell fewer brands but make more money. This refocusing on *power brands* is also going on in P&G, Nestlé, Heinz, and several other companies.

DECIDE WHICH SERVICES TO PRICE AND WHICH TO OFFER FREE

Regarding a company's service mix (e.g., installation, training, delivery), two situations must be avoided. The first is where the company gives away free services that customers take but don't value or even use. This means the company is wasting money on services that are not valued. The second is where the company gives away free products that customers would have been willing to pay for. One solution calls for the company to establish different customer segments, some of which will have to pay for the service and others that will get the service free.

IMPROVE THE PROCESSES FOR CROSS-SELLING AND UPSELLING

Some salespeople resist mentioning other products of their company for a number of reasons. They may be happy with making the sale of their product and don't want to appear pushy. They may not make much or any commission on the other products. They may not think the other products are of sufficiently high quality to satisfy the customer.

The same problem occurs in the professions. A certified public accountant may not recommend that his client use the accounting firm's management consulting service because the accountant doesn't want to risk the client receiving bad service from this other group. Some lawyers will not recommend other law services from their own firm if they don't think highly enough of their fellow lawyers and don't get rewarded anyway.

A department store salesperson who sells a shirt to a customer may not be motivated to suggest other items if he is on straight salary. The customer asked for a shirt. Why exert yourself?

Clearly a company with a range of products needs to supply training and incentives to encourage its staff to promote other products that might interest the customer.

As for upselling, it has two meanings: One is inducing a customer to buy a more expensive version of a product than the one she came to see. The customer came to buy a simple digital camera; she ends up buying a $999 Sony Cyber-shot DSCF717. The other meaning is to approach a customer some years after a purchase and suggest that it is time to replace the old product with a much better one. The seller may even offer a trade-in allowance. Staffs need more skills in both upselling and cross-selling.

Notes

1. Philip Kotler, "Phasing Out Weak Products," *Harvard Business Review* (March–April 1965), pp. 107–118.
2. Marketing Leadership Council, *Stewarding the Brand for Profitable Growth* (Washington, DC: Corporate Executive Board, December 2001), p. 179.

Chapter 8

Your Company's Brand-Building and Communication Skills Are Weak

Signs:

- Your target market does not know much about your company.
- Your brand is not seen as distinctive and better than other brands.
- Your company allocates its budget to the same marketing tools in approximately the same amounts each year.
- You do little evaluation of the ROI impact of your different promotional programs.

YOUR TARGET MARKET DOESN'T KNOW YOU

A company can easily assess whether their communications are paying off by surveying target customers as to their knowledge of and attitudes toward the company. The worst result is where the company has spent a lot of money advertising its name and offerings, but a large number of target customers either never heard of the company or know very little beyond its name and possibly its product area. Less bad but still disturbing is the case where target customers know less than they need to know and even have picked up wrong ideas about the company.

YOUR BRAND LOOKS LIKE ALL THE OTHER BRANDS

Even when a company finds that customers have a fairly good idea of the company's offerings, it may learn that customers don't see much difference between the company's offerings and competitor offerings. Ask this question of customers: "If all competing brands were the same price, which would you buy?" If a customer answers "Any of them" or "I don't have a preference," this is bad news. Or you might ask them, "Describe what you think is distinctive about each brand," and they can't name any differences.

YOUR PROMOTION ALLOCATIONS ARE VIRTUALLY THE SAME EVERY YEAR

When we examine the allocation of promotional money to major communication categories such as advertising, sales promotion, public relations, direct mail, and e-mail, we are likely to find that the proportions remain the same over the years. One reason is that the original allocations led to establishing staffs, relationships, and expectations that tend to persist. Yet we know that the productivity of different communication vehicles and channels changes over time. If the company doesn't change its allocations over time, its marketing productivity will decline.

YOU DON'T EVALUATE THE FINANCIAL IMPACT OF YOUR INVESTMENTS

Marketers tend to think in terms of sales outcomes rather than profit outcomes. Even venturing a sales estimate in connection with some marketing expenditure is done with some hesitation and usually the manager states a range rather than a number. And estimating the profit impact involves a more expert understanding of finance for which marketers are not well equipped.

One reason is that marketing tends to attract people who like to deal with the people world rather than the number world. If a person loved numbers, he or she would probably have gone into finance or accounting. Another problem is that financial projections for marketing expenditures are more difficult than financial projections for capital equipment or other outlays.

Solutions:

- Improve your brand-building strategies and your measurement of results.
- Shift money into those marketing instruments that show increasing effectiveness.
- Develop a financial mindset in the marketers and require them to estimate the ROI impact in advance of their spending requests.

IMPROVE YOUR BRAND-BUILDING STRATEGIES AND MEASURE THE IMPACT ON YOUR BRAND EQUITY

Every company wants to build strong brands. The Interbrand Corporation uses a valuation method of brand equity that leads them to estimate that the Coca-Cola brand, aside from the company's physical assets, was worth $70 billion in 2003.[1] This is followed by nine other global leading brands: Microsoft ($65), IBM ($52), GE ($42), Intel ($31), Nokia ($29), Disney ($28), McDonald's ($25), Marlboro ($22), and Mercedes ($21).

Although Interbrand explains its method of estimating brand equity, Professor Tim Ambler and others take issue with valuation methods of brand equity.[2] One cannot really find out what a brand's equity is worth until there are buyers bidding to buy the brand name. And interested buyers will differ in how much they would offer to buy a brand. Even then, after the brand is purchased, the statement might be made that the buyer paid (say) four times book value, as if this captures the value of the brand itself.

Instead of placing a valuation on the brand, Ambler thinks it is better to monitor selected metrics that would move with brand equity. If the brand commands a larger premium than last year, this is a good sign. If the brand's market share rises, this is a good sign. If target customers say they see rising value in buying and using this brand in relation to competitive brands, this is a good sign.

Each company has to determine the market metrics that indicate increases or decreases in brand equity.

How can companies strengthen their brand equity? Too many marketers think that the magic bullet is advertising. After all, advertising is designed to build more awareness, knowledge, interest, and hopefully preference. But a brand is built by many communication tools, as well as the quality of the product and its packaging, the reliability of the shipping and invoicing, and many other factors. Among the communication tools that create brand impressions, positive or negative, are salespeople, trade shows, social responsibility initiatives, and especially word-of-mouth from customers, competitors, and product reviewers.

In many cases advertising played a very small role in the success of companies: McDonald's in the early days relied more on public relations and Starbucks and Wal-Mart grew by word-of-mouth.

The fact is that a brand evokes a set of customer expectations. Brand equity results from how well customer expectations are fulfilled. The higher the satisfaction, the higher the brand equity. And the higher the perceived value of the offering, the higher the brand equity.

SHIFT MONEY INTO MARKETING INSTRUMENTS OF GREATER EFFECTIVENESS

Marketing tools change in their cost effectiveness over time. When TV advertising first appeared, it was considerably more effective than radio advertising for many classes of products. TV advertising was extremely effective from the 1960s through the mid-1980s. But a new book by Al and Laura Ries published in 2002 carried the challenging title: *The Fall of Advertising and the Rise of PR.*[3] If the Rieses are correct, today's marketers should shift more of their budget to public relations.

Then we notice that telemarketing kept growing in the 1990s and early 2000s, implying growing effectiveness. But in July 2003, the U.S. government decided to pass a law that made it easy for consumers to delist themselves from receiving telemarketing calls with a penalty of $11,000 per call per offender.

Given that marketing tools change in their cost effectiveness over time, why do so many companies make the same budget allocations over time? Is it laziness, disbelief, or incompetence? Clearly companies court marketing waste when they stick to old budget allocations.

Let's examine the changing efficiencies of some major marketing tools.

Advertising

The old saw of John Wanamaker, who said, "Half of my advertising is wasted but I don't know which half," still applies today, especially in connection with mass advertising. Does Coca-Cola need to put another ad showing its bottle on the back cover of a magazine at a cost of $80,000 when most people know about Coca-Cola and most people probably won't pay attention to the ad? And what if they did? The ad doesn't convey any new information or benefit. And do women remember the 30-second TV commercial for a new skin cream when the commercial was tucked between five other equally brief commercials?

Most companies spend money in this way because they have done this in the past and feel that it is too risky to do otherwise. They see spending money on costly ads as a form of insurance that the company will be remembered even when it has nothing new to say and no new way of saying it. The real question companies should ask is whether the same amount of money would work better if spent on improving the product's quality or customer service or on better logistics. Remember that advertising is a cost that the customers pay and maybe many of them would prefer a lower price. Given that the average General Motors car consumes $3,000 in advertising cost, how many more cars could GM sell if it reduced its price by $3,000 a car?

Some ad campaigns admittedly are effective and boost the company's sales. People wouldn't have been so excited to pay a higher price for Absolut Vodka than Smirnoff Vodka if it wasn't for Absolut's brilliant ad campaign. But how many advertising campaigns are brilliant? Most are at best average! In fact, some ads cannot even be deciphered as to the point they are making.

So why are many ad campaigns average? Ask the ad

agency and it will blame the brand manager who wants to play safe and therefore tames the bold ad into a safe one. Ask the brand manager who claims that the ad agency didn't come up with a great ad idea.

I advise brand managers to ask their agency for three different ad campaign ideas, going from mild to wild. A better answer might be for the company not to go to only one agency for creative ideas, but instead pay several agencies to compete to deliver a great ad idea.

Ads work better when they are placed in the media read by the target market. Find the magazines read by fishermen, motorcycle enthusiasts, hobbyists, mechanical engineers—and advertise products of interest to them and the ads will be read. The ads usually carry response cards for readers to get further information or place orders, making ROI measurement much easier.

Measuring advertising's financial impact is most directly accomplishable with direct marketing campaigns when the advertiser can trace the number of orders resulting from a specific campaign having a certain cost.

Sales Promotion

Most sales promotion programs are unprofitable! One extensive study of sales promotion programs concluded that only 17 percent were profitable. The most unprofitable sales promotion program is one where only the current users end up buying the product on sale. No new customers tried the product. This amounts to giving the current customers a subsidy that leads them to buy more units this period and fewer units next period.

The second-worst case is where the sales promotion attracts some new triers but they come from the ranks of the deal-prone price shoppers who never remain loyal to any brand. The company attracted incremental sales, but just for the period.

The best sales promotion occurs when the campaign attracts many new triers who find the brand to be superior and they make it their preferred brand. This happens only if the brand has been a sleeper in that it is superior to the other brands but was not well known to the consumers. In this case, the company would be advised to distribute samples and not just rely on sales promotion as the stimulus.

Too often sales promotions are developed by brand managers with little experience in what constitutes effective promotions. One solution is to appoint an experienced sales promotion person to advise others on best promotions. This person would also analyze the results of each promotion to further learn what works best. Alternatively, the company should hire a sales promotion agency that can professionally recommend the best promotion to use under different circumstances.

Public Relations

There is a growing belief that public relations, long treated as an orphan in the promotion mix, deserves growing use relative to the advertising budget. Public relations is a better audience-building tool particularly with new high-tech products where buyers want independent professional opinion before they choose a brand. The maker of a high-tech product should first identify opinion leaders—key experts, columnists, and others—who review and talk about new products. For example, Walter S. Mossberg of the *Wall Street Journal* writes an influential column evaluating new products. Many customers value his recommendations.

Consider how Volvo launched its new SUV using PR rather than advertising first.

> *Volvo launched its new SUV, the XC90, with a PR campaign instead of a big-budget advertising splurge. Its marketers identified key journalists and involved them early in the development process. Later these journalists previewed the finished car with the designers, engineers, and safety experts. They drove the car and wrote many stories that reached key influentials. This created a huge buzz that resulted in pre-sales of 7,500 vehicles and won Volvo the North American Truck of the Year and* Motor Trend's *SUV of the Year awards, much of this occurring before any money was spent on ads.*

Direct Marketing

Companies that can sell direct to their customers and prospects enjoy a considerable advantage. They don't have to pay commissions to intermediaries or lose sight of who is actually buying their products. They don't have to fill the intermediaries' pipelines but base their production more on what's directly coming in as orders.

Dell Computer became the world's leading personal computer manufacturer by selling direct. Initially they took orders by phone but today they get virtually 90 percent of the orders online. Customers specify what computer features they want and send their credit card information to Dell. Dell immediately orders any components they need from suppliers. They assemble the new computer and ship it in a few days. Meanwhile Dell received payment immediately but doesn't pay its suppliers for 60 days, resulting in money being made from the float as well as from the price. Dell has inspired other companies to move from "producing for stock" to "producing for orders."

REQUIRE MARKETERS TO SUPPLY ESTIMATES OF THE FINANCIAL IMPACT OF THEIR SPENDING REQUESTS

Senior management are becoming impatient with marketing budget requests from marketers who do not supply an estimate of the financial impact of their planned expenditure. Furthermore, senior management don't even get an after-the-fact estimate of the actual financial impact.

At Coca-Cola, senior management is beginning to insist that these before-and-after estimates be supplied. They know that marketers are making a guess, but hopefully an educated guess. Coca-Cola's real purpose is to produce a *financial mindset* in its marketers. It wants its marketers to become familiar with margins, asset turnover, ROI, economic value added, and shareholder value. The more that marketers get to think in financial terms, the better the dialog that will take place between the marketing and financial people.

Notes

1. "Brands in an Age of Anti-Americanism," *Business Week*, August 4, 2003, pp. 69–78.
2. Tim Ambler, *Marketing and the Bottom Line*, 2nd ed. (London: FT Prentice Hall, 2003).
3. Al Ries and Laura Ries, *The Fall of Advertising and the Rise of PR* (New York: HarperBusiness, 2002).

Chapter 9

Your Company Is Not Well Organized to Carry On Effective and Efficient Marketing

Signs:

- The head of marketing does not seem to be very effective.
- The staff lacks some marketing skills needed in the twenty-first century.
- There are bad vibes between marketing/sales and the other departments.

THE HEAD OF MARKETING DOES NOT SEEM TO BE VERY EFFECTIVE

An effective *chief marketing officer* (CMO) has three jobs. The first is to run the marketing department well, hiring competent staff, setting high standards for marketing planning and implementation, improving the staff's skills at research, forecasting, and communication. The second task is to win the confidence of the heads of other departments—finance, operations, purchasing, information technology, and so on—and to get the whole organization to serve and satisfy the customers. A third task is to work well with the CEO and deliver on the CEO's expectations regarding growth and profitability.

A few CMOs are competent at all three tasks; some are competent at two tasks; and too many may fail at all three tasks. In the latter cases, it is time to find a new CMO.

THE MARKETING DEPARTMENT LACKS CONTEMPORARY SKILLS

Marketing departments have traditionally practiced four skills: marketing research, advertising, sales promotion, and sales management. These are traditional skills and scores of books have been written about each. Yet many departments are deficient in even these skills, let alone a set of new skills that are required to deal with twenty-first-century marketing challenges.

STRAINED RELATIONS BETWEEN MARKETING AND THE OTHER DEPARTMENTS

It would take a brief set of interviews to establish how well the marketing people are respected or disrespected by the staffs in other departments of the company. The other departments frequently complain about various practices of the marketing department. And the marketing people will point out many faults and frictions in their relationship with the other departments.

Solutions:

- Appoint a stronger leader of the marketing department.
- Build new skills in the marketing department.
- Improve marketing's relations with the other departments.

APPOINT A STRONGER LEADER OF THE MARKETING DEPARTMENT

Marketing vice presidents come from a variety of backgrounds: advertising, sales, new products, sometimes engineering or finance. They bring their biases with them. The hope is that they will take a more holistic view of marketing principles, tools, and processes and establish a good balance among them.

The CMO's challenge is to gain the respect of the CEO and various department heads and employees throughout the company. This will happen if marketing's forecasts are fairly accurate, and there is accountability for the marketing expenditures in terms of their contribution to ROI or other financial measures.

Herb Kelleher, the brilliant co-founder of Southwest Airlines, went so far as to rename the marketing department: "We don't have a Marketing Department; we have a Customer Department." And in the words of an enlightened Ford executive, "If we're not customer driven, our cars won't be either."

BUILD NEW SKILLS IN THE MARKETING DEPARTMENT

Today's marketing environment is much more challenging than ever, with its haunting overcapacity, hypercompetition, and falling margins. Marketers need to try new initiatives and acquire new skills. These new skills are described below.

New Marketing Skills

- Positioning.
- Brand asset management.
- Customer relationship management (CRM) and database marketing.
- Partner relationship management (PRM).
- Company contact center.
- Internet marketing.
- Public relations marketing.
- Service and experiential marketing.
- Integrated marketing communications.
- Profitability analysis.
- Market-driving skills.

Positioning

Al Ries and Jack Trout introduced the concept of brand positioning in 1982 and it is a central concept in marketing.[1] They asserted that each brand should *own* a *word*: Volvo owns "safety" and BMW owns "driving performance" and Tide owns "Cleans cleanest." They argue that no brand should come into the market as a me-too brand. A new brand should offer an important new benefit and therefore create a new category. Don't come in second in a category; always come in first in a new category.

Positioning thinking evolved further when Michael Treacy and Fred Wiersema wrote *The Discipline of Market Leaders*.[2] They distinguished between three basic positionings: product leadership, operational excellence, and customer intimacy. A competitor can opt for the product leadership position, always leading the other firms in advancing the quality and performance of the product. A second competitor could lead the others in operational excellence, excelling in cost management and service reliability. A third competitor could claim the position of customer intimacy, knowing more about each customer's needs and varying their offerings accordingly. In the aerospace business, GE claims the position as "product leader." In the fast-food business, McDonald's claims "operational excellence" while Burger King claims "customer intimacy" (or "Have it Your Way").

Treacy and Wiersema claim that companies typically cannot excel in all three ways, first because this would be too costly and second because the three positions contain contradictions. Thus if McDonald's wants to be both operationally excellent and customer intimate, these would conflict: customers who wanted the hamburger cooked differently would slow down the lines and McDonald's operational excellence, based on standardization, would suffer.

So Treacy and Wiersema's message is to lead in one of these three positionings and be at least at the average level in the other two positionings. Don't fall below average in the other two! Customers may want to buy from the product leader but will drop this supplier if its reliability is poor or it refuses to modify its offerings.

More recently, Crawford and Mathews offered another formula for positioning. They see firms positioned along five attributes: *product*, *price*, *ease of access*, *value-added service*, and *customer experience*.[3] They assert that a company will be most profitable if it *dominates* on one of these attributes, performs above average (*differentiates*) along a second, and is at *industry par* with the remaining three. They advise that it is too costly for a company to try to be great in all five ways. As an example, Wal-Mart dominates in low prices, is above average in product range, and is quite average in ease of access, value-added service, and customer experience.

Clearly further ideas will evolve on the subject of positioning. My observation is that too many brands are still weakly positioned and sound very much like their competitors, in which case positioning remains a badly needed skill.

Brand Asset Management

Brand asset management is closely related to positioning. Certain brands are so central to a company's current and future performance that they need to be managed, enhanced, and protected as an asset. Brand names such as Coca-Cola, Sony, Intel, and Disney can be extended into new products, product variants, and services. And someone has to police the use to which such "star power" names are put. None of these firms can let a cheap or disappointing product be launched under its name. Disney cannot risk operating poorly managed stores or hotels. Coca-Cola cannot use its name for a new detergent or theme park. These names are well-positioned and deviations from the positioning center of these brands must be avoided.

Customer Relationship Management (CRM) and Database Marketing

Companies can improve their targeting precision by collecting information about their individual customers. By building a customer database that contains past transactions, demographics, psychographics, and other useful information, the company will be in a much better position to match offers to individuals. Beyond this, skilled statisticians can mine the customer data to discern new segments and trends that point to new opportunities. The customer database can be accessed by managers in market planning, merchandising, product development, customer rewards, channel management, sales analysis, cross-selling, and promotion analysis. CRM skills are rapidly being added in marketing departments to create a competitive advantage over competitors who work at a grosser level of analysis.

Partner Relationship Management (PRM)

As more companies perform more of their activities through partners, the skill of managing partner relationships becomes critical. The productivity of partners depends on their feeling satisfied with the terms of the relationship and the opportunities that will come their way in working closely with the company. The company needs to periodically take the temperature of each major partner, and respond quickly to any signs of dissatisfaction or distancing. A company should appoint someone to manage supplier relations and another to manage distributor relations, very much like the human resource department manages employee relations. Beyond this, individual managers should manage each significant partner and develop a plan for strengthening ties and performance.

Company Contact Center

A company needs to consolidate its activities for reaching, listening to, and learning about customers in what has been described as a *contact center* (or *customer interaction center*). The contact center was originally the company's telephone system, which brought in incoming calls and also was used for telemarketing purposes. Today, companies need to integrate all the information coming from "customer touchpoints," such as the telephone, regular mail, e-mail, faxes, and store visits. In this way, the company can capture information that will provide a 360-degree view of the individual customer.

The failure to integrate customer information was dramatized to me by the CEO of a large company who received a dunning letter from his bank about not making his mortgage payment. This CEO was well-known to the commercial section of the bank but not known to the consumer mortgage group. Apparently the CEO's wife forgot to make a mortgage payment in the previous month. The CEO withdrew all his commercial business from this bank.

The company's telephone lines are becoming increasingly critical to serving customers well. Customers need to be able to reach a company with questions, orders, and complaints. Answering questions well, taking down orders accurately, and resolving complaints quickly are important skills. Every call can yield valuable information to add to the customer's file in the database and can also occasion a sales message.

The phone is also important to use for outbound telemarketing campaigns. Much design goes into getting access to a set of prospect phone numbers and knowing when to call and what to say. A company can quickly assess its telemarketing effectiveness by the purchase response rate that it achieves with its calls.

So important is the telephone operation to effective marketing that many companies have outsourced this operation to professional telemarketers. In Japan, companies such as Sony, Sharp, Toshiba, and many others have outsourced the management of their customer telephone operations to Bell 24, a major outsourcer.

One of the negative ways companies are currently handling their telephone operations is overautomating the telephone-answering system, where the customer hears several options, chooses one, only to hear another set of options, and on and on, with no chance of reaching a live operator, resulting in a lost service opportunity and maybe a lost customer. Although telephone automation delivers lower costs, which pleases the company's financial types, there is failure to recognize the greater costs in lost customer sales and satisfaction. A useful resolution is to make sure that callers know that at any time they can hit zero and reach a live operator.

Internet Marketing

Virtually all companies have created their own web site where viewers can learn about the company's product line, history, philosophies, job opportunities, and recent news about the company. Some companies go further and use their web site as a sales channel, as does Dell Computer, Amazon, W.W. Grainger, and scores of other companies that sell over the Internet.

But there are many additional marketing applications that most companies have not yet tapped: market research, competitive intelligence, concept and product testing, coupon and sampling distribution, product customization, and employee and dealer training. The key need is for the company to add Internet-savvy individuals to further exploit the potentials of the Internet.

Public Relations Marketing

Public relations, long the stepchild of the promotion mix, is now coming into more prominence. Some years ago, Tom Harris wrote a book called *A Marketer's Guide to Public Relations* that underscored how many clever PR campaigns, and not advertising, deserved the credit for creating many product successes.[4] Tom was a partner in the PR firm of Golin-Harris and this firm was largely responsible for McDonald's PR from the time of McDonald's lowly beginnings. In many ways, McDonald's is a PR success story, with its children's hospital, children's playgrounds, charitable contributions, sponsorships, and Golden Arches.

High-tech firms discovered early that PR skills are critical to spreading information about a new product. Firms would submit their new high-tech products to well-known reviewers in the hope of receiving a highly positive recommendation. Their PR departments would assiduously cultivate press attention to circulate positive stories about the product in addition to creating high-profile events and sponsorships.

The most recent case for the important role of PR is found in Al and Laura Ries's new book, *The Fall of Advertising and the Rise of PR*. The Rieses have repositioned PR as a communication tool to be used in the early stages of the commercial launch process while advertising should be used in the later stages.

The main point here is that companies need to add PR skills in the marketing department and not rely on begging and borrowing them on an as-needed basis from the company's PR department or agency.

Service and Experiential Marketing

Outstanding service can be a powerful differentiator in the absence of other differentiators. Leonard Berry, one of the leading experts on service marketing, personally interviewed several companies that were widely praised for their outstanding service—companies such as The Container Store, Charles Schwab Corporation, Chick-fil-A, Custom Research, Enterprise Rent-A-Car, and USAA—in his quest to improve our understanding of service marketing.[5] He found the most salient practices to be:

- Values-driven leadership.
- Strategic focus.
- Executional excellence.
- Control of destiny.
- Trust-based relationships.
- Investment in employee success.
- Acting small.
- Brand cultivation.
- Generosity.

Service marketing has been lifted to a new level by the recent work on *experience marketing*. Joe Pine and James Gilmore think that companies should develop skill in designing marketing *experiences*.[6] The idea has many sources. Great restaurants are known for the "customer experience" as much as for their food. Restaurants such as Planet Hollywood and Hard Rock Café were specifically set up to deliver a special experience. Starbucks charges us $2 or more to experience coffee in a special setting. Las Vegas hotels, anxious to distinguish themselves, take on the character of Ancient Rome or

Venice or New York. But the "experience" master is Walt Disney, who created park simulations of the cowboy West, fairyland castles, pirate ships, and the like. The aim of the experiential marketer is to add drama and entertainment to what otherwise might pass as stale fare.

> *Thus we enter Niketown to buy basketball shoes and confront a 15-foot photo of Michael Jordan. We proceed to the basketball court to test if Nike's shoes help us score more baskets. Or we enter REI, an outdoor equipment store, and test out climbing equipment on their climbing wall, or test out a rainproof coat by going under a simulated rainfall. Or we enter Bass Pro to buy a fishing rod and test it by casting in their fish pool.*

All merchants offer services; your challenge is to escort your customer through a memorable experience.

Integrated Marketing Communications

Among the most important skills in marketing are communication and promotion. Communication is the broader term and it happens whether planned or not. A salesperson's clothes communicate, the catalog communicates, the company's office decor communicates . . . all create impressions on the receiving party. This explains the growing interest in *Integrated Marketing Communications* (IMC).[7] Companies need to orchestrate a consistent set of impressions from their personnel, facilities, and actions that deliver the company's brand meaning and promise to its various audiences. It all starts with defining the company's values and making sure that they are understood and exemplified by all of the company's employees.

Profitability Analysis

Most companies do not know their real profitability by geographies, products, segments, customers, and channels. They too often assume that their profits are proportional to their sales volume but this ignores the different margins and different costs. For example, many companies no longer believe that their largest customers are their most profitable customers. Large customers often demand the lowest prices and considerable services. Some mid-sized customers are more profitable measured as a rate of return on the cost of serving them. Company accounting departments, while ready to conduct deep analyses of production costs and variances, are less willing or able to accumulate the costs of serving various marketing entities and subtracting these costs from the respective revenue streams. Thus two customers spending the same amount may yield different profits. If one customer keeps phoning the company, asking for discounts, consuming many more company services, and paying its bills late, it is less profitable than the second company that does none of this.

Fortunately Robert Kaplan and Robin Cooper outlined a correct approach to accounting for profitability with their Activity-Based Costing (ABC) accounting.[8] The method would require salespeople to report how much time and expense each customer consumed, much like lawyers bill clients for each half hour of their time and expense.

All said, marketers must add profit measurement and financial skills to increase the marketing department's accountability for their budget allocations over geographies, products, segments, customers, and channels.

Market-Driving Skills

Effective marketing has traditionally been defined as the ability to "find needs and fill them." This defines a *market-driven firm*. But with so many needs now being filled by countless products, the challenge now is to invent new needs. This is the goal of a *market-driving firm*. As Sony's visionary leader, Akio Morita, put it: "Our plan is to lead the public with new products rather than ask them what kinds of products they want. The public does not know what is possible, but we do." And according to an executive at 3M, "Our goal is to lead customers where they want to go before *they* know where they want to go."[9]

Market-driving firms revolutionize their industries by creating a *new value proposition* and/or a *new business system* that offers leaps in benefits and/or reductions in acquisitions efforts/costs. Many competitors may imitate the new value proposition but tend to be less successful in copying the business system. Market-driving firms have these characteristics:[10]

- Guiding by vision rather than by traditional market research (FedEx, Body Shop, Swatch).
- Redrawing industry segmentation (Southwest, Wal-Mart, SAP).
- Creating value through new price points (Southwest, Charles Schwab, and Wal-Mart created lower prices; CNN, Starbucks, and FedEx set higher prices).
- Growing sales through customer education (IKEA).
- Reconfiguring channels (FedEx, Southwest, Benetton).
- Using the buzz network (Southwest, Club Med, Virgin).
- Overwhelming customer expectations (FedEx, Home Depot, Southwest).

IMPROVE THE RELATIONS BETWEEN MARKETING AND THE OTHER DEPARTMENTS

Another initiative to build a stronger marketing department is to improve marketing's relationship with every other department. We will examine the relationships shown below.

Marketing Relationships with Other Departments

- Marketing and sales.
- Marketing, R&D, and engineering.
- Marketing and manufacturing.
- Marketing and purchasing.
- Marketing and accounting.
- Marketing and finance.
- Marketing and logistics.

Marketing and Sales

It may be surprising to say that marketing must improve its relations with the sales department. In most companies, the two departments are headed by different vice presidents. Marketing typically takes care of product planning, market planning, pricing, lead generation, and communications. Sales takes care of reaching and developing customers and getting orders. Various frictions can arise. The sales vice president may urge marketing to lower prices, or request a larger share of the budget to hire more salespeople or pay them more. The marketing vice president may prefer to use the money for stronger communications to build the brand and pull in demand and may justify the higher prices as a way to pay for the communication costs.

The central question is whether the two vice presidents respect each other and try to objectively (not politically) determine the best division of the marketing/sales resources. This underscores the need to develop more accountability overall for marketing/sales expenditures, so issues can be settled on harder evidence of effectiveness.

Other measures will also improve the relationship between marketing and salespeople. First, the marketing planning process must include one or more salespeople involved in the process so that they have their say and buy into the plan. Second, the relationship will be improved if marketing people regularly get out of their offices and travel with salespeople to meet customers and understand the customers and the salespeople better. Marketers can make better decisions if they regard the salespeople as their immediate customers who also must be satisfied.

Marketing, R&D, and Engineering

Marketing's only issue with R&D is when they are not invited in early enough in the planning of new products. In designing new products, scientists and engineers will make a lot of assumptions about customers and market forces without sufficient investigation. They might over-design the product, causing its price to be too high; or they may describe the product in too technical a language that emphasizes features rather than benefits. All this can be improved by marketers working closely with R&D and engineers to supply consumer guidance based on hard data.

Marketing and Manufacturing

Marketing often interferes with the smooth operation of production. Marketing may plan a special promotion that requires manufacturing to schedule increased production work and this may involve working overtime at higher cost. Or marketing may request smaller batches of product for special markets and this requires manufacturing to reset their tools and dies.

Who should prevail? The question is one of estimating the increased revenue flowing from these requests against the increased costs. If marketing's requests lead to higher profits, then their view should prevail. When this is less certain, it is sometimes better for marketing not to make demands on manufacturing until they really can have a big win.

Marketing and Purchasing

Marketing has built brands that make quality promises. Purchasing has to meet the expected quality standards.

Yet purchasing is tempted to bring down costs. If purchasing chooses poorer or slower suppliers, marketing's promises to the customers will not be realized. Marketing needs to develop good relations with the purchasing people to insure that the quality standards are met.

Marketing and Accounting

Marketers could have a number of concerns about the accounting department. The company accountants are responsible for sending out invoices and collecting receivables. If customers call and complain that invoices are inaccurate or difficult to understand, do the accountants answer quickly? If clients are late in their payments, do the accountants handle this carefully or harass them? Do the accountants prepare useful studies of profitability by geographical areas, products, market segments, customers, and channels?

Marketing and Finance

The big issue between marketing and finance concerns marketing's accountability for the financial impact of its expenditures. Without a strong case by marketing that requested funds would produce measurable profit, finance is less willing to grant the funds. Finance also is careful about accepting new customers whose credit is questionable. The sales force thinks that the credit people within finance are too conservative and undermining their commissions by rejecting some new business.

Marketing and Logistics

To get orders, salespeople typically make promises regarding delivery times. Late deliveries can alienate the customers. Sometimes the fault may lie with purchasing or manufacturing. Or it may lie with the inventory group or the shipping department. Marketers have a stake in the reliable performance of the people involved in logistics.

Notes

1. Al Ries and Jack Trout, *Positioning: The Battle for Your Mind* (New York: Warner Books, 1982).
2. Michael Treacy and Fred Wiersema, *The Discipline of Market Leaders* (Reading, MA: Addison-Wesley, 1994).
3. Fred Crawford and Ryan Mathews, *The Myth of Excellence: Why Great Companies Never Try to Be the Best at Everything* (New York: Crown Business, 2001).
4. Thomas L. Harris, *The Marketer's Guide to Public Relations* (New York: John Wiley & Sons, 1991).
5. Leonard J. Berry, *Discovering the Soul of Service* (New York: Free Press, 1999).

6. B. Joseph Pine II and James H. Gilmore, *The Experience Economy: Work Is Theatre & Every Business a Stage* (Boston: Harvard Business School Press, 1999).
7. Don E. Schultz, Stanley I. Tannenbaum, and Robert F. Lauterborn, *Integrated Marketing Communications* (Lincolnwood, IL: NTC Business Books, 1993).
8. Robert S. Kaplan and Robin Cooper, *Cost & Effect: Using Integrated Cost Systems to Drive Profitability and Performance* (Boston: Harvard Business School Press, 1998).
9. See Gary Hamel and C.K. Prahalad, "Seeing the Future First," *Fortune*, September 5, 1994, pp. 64–70; Philip Kotler, *Kotler on Marketing* (New York: Free Press, 1999), pp. 20–24; and Anthony W. Ulwick, "Turn Customer Input Into Innovation," *Harvard Business Review*, January 2002, pp. 91–97.
10. Nirmalya Kumar, Philip Kotler, and Lisa Sheer, "Market Driving Companies," *European Management Journal*, April 2000, pp. 129–142.

Chapter 10

Your Company Has Not Made Maximum Use of Technology

Signs:

- The company has made minimal use of the Internet.
- The company's sales automation system is outdated.
- The company has not introduced any market automation.
- The marketing group lacks decision-support models.
- The marketing group needs to develop marketing dashboards.

INSUFFICIENT USE OF THE INTERNET

Many companies think that they are using the Internet because they have established a web site(s) and may even sell online. But this represents only 10 percent of the opportunities afforded by the Internet.

SALES AUTOMATION SYSTEM IS DEFICIENT

Salespeople normally use a software program to remember things about their customers. But the software programs continue to improve and must be updated.

NO EXAMPLES OF MARKET AUTOMATION

Some marketing decisions can be made more easily or better by software than by human decision making; yet too few companies have used marketing automation.

FEW FORMAL DECISION MODELS

Most marketing decisions are still made intuitively. Yet company decisions can benefit from the construction and use of formal marketing decision models.

LITTLE USE OF MARKETING DASHBOARDS

Marketing is increasingly a game won by the competitor possessing better information. The information can be codified and made available to managers through standard computer screen *dashboards*. Today's dashboards are relatively primitive in relation to what potentially can be done.

Solutions:

- Make more use of the Internet.
- Improve the sales automation system.
- Apply market automation to routine marketing decisions.
- Develop some formal marketing decision models.
- Develop marketing dashboards.

EXPLOIT THE INTERNET

The Internet has many more uses than companies commonly know. Here are the major uses.

An Effective Web Site

The most important marketing use of the Internet is the establishment of an effective and attractive web site describing the company, its products, its distributors, its job opportunities, and its officers. Not all web sites are user-friendly or effective. The download time could be excessive because of overly fancy graphics. It might be confusing to navigate to new pages or to make payment for a purchase on the Internet. The web site might lack the kind of information that would draw visitors back again. The web site might be bland like many others and fail to convey the company's personality.

It is a fairly straightforward matter to assess the effectiveness of your company's web site. The main group to survey is your customers. What is their experience with the web site and what are their suggestions for improvement? The other source is to invite web site experts to give their assessment and suggestions for improvement.

Companies need to figure out how to add value to their web sites that will draw visitors back again. For example, Sony uses its www.PlayStation.com web site to build relationships with game-players of all ages. The site offers information about the latest games, news about events and promotions, game guides and support, and even online forums in which game-players can swap tips and stories.

An Effective Intranet

Your company needs to use the intranet as an efficient communication tool within the company. Employees must be able to reach each other by e-mail, to download documents from the company's mainframe, and to upload sales and other reports to the mainframe.

Effective Extranets

Companies are increasingly linking themselves electronically to their main suppliers, distributors, and dealers. They are using the Internet as a platform for these connections. Thus a company like Ford can send orders for needed auto parts to its suppliers without having to phone or mail paper documents. Ford can also send funds to the supplier's banks in payment for its parts. Ford can also send information to its dealers on a daily basis with selling suggestions, price changes, car searches, and so on. In all these cases, companies can save considerable money and time by investing in electronic links with their key suppliers, distributors, and dealers.

E-Training Online

All companies must keep their employees up-to-date with the latest knowledge and skills for running their business. In the past this meant bringing their people together in a central location and running a several-day training session. The companies would bear high travel and hotel costs and lost production and selling time. Thanks to the Internet, companies are increasingly developing training materials for online viewing on the Internet with passwords. Employees will be expected to give time to reading the material and taking tests. IBM, for example, now runs 25 percent of its training online, saving millions of dollars.

E-Recruitment

The Internet has facilitated companies searching for talent. This occurs in two ways. The company can post job openings on its own web site. It can also utilize job market Internet sites such as Monster.com in trying to fill job vacancies.

E-Procurement

The quickest way that a company can save money is for its purchasing people to start buying their inputs on the Internet. Companies can use the Internet to identify new sources of supply; to compare prices; to go on bidding sites for new or used products; and to announce their own needs and request bids. E-procurement brings down the costs because of the lessened need to deal with salespeople and the greater price transparency available to buyers.

E-Market Research

The Internet provides an information highway that is a boon to market researchers. A company can learn a great deal about its competitors by designating that all news items about specific competitors be gathered in one site. The company's market researchers can run online focus groups, consumer panels, and dealer panels to test new product, service, and communication ideas. The company can send out differentiated offers to similar groups and measure the response difference. The company can offer coupons and samples and check whether they lead to purchases. All said, the company's marketing research skills are enhanced manyfold by the use of the Internet.

E-Chat Rooms

Some companies may want to add a chat room to their web site in order to build a *brand community* where their customers and fans can exchange ideas and information. This works well with companies such as Apple Computer or Harley Davidson, whose customers enjoy meeting and learning from each other. E-chat rooms are not a good idea for companies that don't fully satisfy their customers and will probably draw some unsavory criticism. Companies would be wise to audit other chat rooms dealing with their product area to learn from them.

IMPROVE YOUR SALES AUTOMATION SYSTEM

Your sales force should be equipped with the latest sales automation system. The system should enable them to answer any questions in the prospect's or customer's office and empower them to make decisions on behalf of the company. Thus a prospect may show an interest in the salesperson's proposal. However, he might say that he would need delivery in three days. Using the sales automation system, the salesperson clicks on her company's inventory situation and reports that a delivery could actually be made in two days. The prospect is pleased but he hesitates: "I need a better price." The salesperson hits her sales automation system and says: "I don't want you to lose the order. I can cut the price by two percent. But that is all I can do." "Good," says the prospect, but he still hesitates. "I don't like the liability provision in the fourth paragraph of the contract. It must be modified." The salesperson suggests a change in the paragraph to which the prospect agrees. At last the prospect places the order and signs the contract.

All said, the sales automation system enables salespeople to possess the knowledge needed to make profitable decisions on behalf of the company.

USE MORE MARKET AUTOMATION

A number of routine marketing decisions can be better handled by software than by company personnel. The company makes better decisions and saves on labor time. The fact that software can beat human decision making is well-illustrated by IBM's Deep Blue software beating the world's greatest living chess champion, Gary Kasparov. If software can be developed to handle such a complex game as chess, certainly it can be developed for some routine marketing decisions. Here are two examples:

1. Airlines would like to sell as many seats on a prospective flight as possible before the plane takes off. Almost anything they can get for an otherwise-unsold seat will exceed the cost. The airlines use software programs to guide *yield-based pricing*. The software programs determine when the price of a seat should be lowered before a flight and sends the information to travel agents and certain customers. An airline as

large as American prefers to trust the software program to having several employees involved full time in changing airline fares.

2. Choosing positions for brands on a shelf can now be better accomplished with software than guesswork. Kraft manages the cheese category for many stores, and can determine the best mix of cheese brands and their shelf positionings for stores in low-, medium-, and high-income areas.

In the future, we can expect companies to invest further in automating their routine marketing decisions.

DEVELOP DECISION SUPPORT MODELS

Since the 1960s, academic marketers have been developing marketing decision support models. They go under such names as CALLPLAN, DETAILER, MEDIAC, PROMOTER, and so on.[1] Each model dealt with a specific marketing decision area. Today firms are also trying their hand at *marketing mix modeling* that combines the separate and collective effects of a marketing mix on sales and profits. A company can get help in developing these and other models from a variety of marketing resource management vendors such as Veridiem or Marketing Management Analytics.

DEVELOP MARKETING DASHBOARDS

We drive our automobiles with the help of the dials on a dashboard. Consider an airplane taking off at night, flying up 30,000 feet, and later landing safely, where the only guide to the pilot is the dashboard. This is *flying by wire*, that is, flying only with information. Can a firm also guide its flight toward its objectives primarily by relying on current information on its dashboard?

We can discern three types of dashboards coming into use:

1. A *marketing performance dashboard* that reports where the company now stands in relation to its objectives. Included would be latest data on sales, market shares, costs, and prices of the company and its competitors. Red flags would indicate underachievement. The user can drill down further into any number to analyze what might account for any underachievement. The user might find that one of the three salespeople in the Chicago area has fallen way behind in meeting his quotas. This is a signal to contact him and determine what has happened and whether it can be corrected.
2. A *marketing processes dashboard* that coaches users on how to carry out any marketing process in a best-of-class way. Thus a new brand manager might want to do a concept test. She types in *concept test* and the

computer screen shows that a concept test has four steps. For each step, an example is supplied with tips on how to do it efficiently. In essence, a mentor has been put into the computer to guide brand managers. Other processes would be market testing, choosing a new advertising agency, and so on. P&G has done work to codify all of its processes in this way.

3. A *marketing tools dashboard* that contains statistical programs that can be applied to data sets to find means, standard deviations, cross-tabulations, regression analysis, discriminant analysis, factor analysis, cluster analysis, and so on. Suites of the more useful programs are commercially available from SAS and other companies.

Note

1. See Philip Kotler, *Marketing Management*, 11th ed. (Upper Saddle River, NJ: Prentice-Hall, 2003), p. 141.

Epilogue

The Ten Commandments of Marketing Effectiveness

The theory of marketing is solid but the practice of marketing leaves much to be desired. I have listed the ten deadly sins, deficits, weaknesses, call-it-what-you-will, of marketing as practiced. I have described the main signs of each sin and proposed solutions. Applying the solutions will turn the ten sins into the *ten commandments for attaining high marketing productivity and profitability*. The ten commandments are listed below. Frame them and hang them on your walls!

1. The company segments the market, chooses the best segments, and develops a strong position in each chosen segment.
2. The company maps its customers' needs, perceptions, preferences, and behavior and motivates its stakeholders to obsess about serving and satisfying the customers.
3. The company knows its major competitors and their strengths and weaknesses.
4. The company builds partners out of its stakeholders and generously rewards them.
5. The company develops systems for identifying opportunities, ranking them, and choosing the best ones.
6. The company manages a marketing planning system that leads to insightful long-term and short-term plans.

7. The company exercises strong control over its product and service mix.
8. The company builds strong brands by using the most cost-effective communication and promotion tools.
9. The company builds marketing leadership and a team spirit among its various departments.
10. The company constantly adds technology that gives it a competitive advantage in the marketplace.

Index

Absolut Vodka, 97
Accounting and marketing departments, 125
Activity-Based Costing accounting, 120
Advertising, 95–98
Amazon, 27, 115
Apple Computer, 136–137

Becton-Dickenson, 79–80
Benetton, 121
BMW, 109
Body Shop, 121
Brand asset management, 111
Brand-building skills
  allocations to marketing tools and, 96–101
  brand equity, market metrics, and, 94–95
  distinctiveness and, 92
  financial projections and, 93, 101–102
  signs of problems with, 91
  solutions to problems with, 93
  target market and, 91
Brands, 5–6, 85–86
"Bringing Silicon Valley Inside Your Company" (Hamel), 67
Budgeting, flexible, 78–79
Burger King, 109
Business strategy, marketing as driving, 3, 9

Cannibalizing self, 49, 50
Caterpillar, 60–61
CEO and marketing costs, 4–5
Challenges of marketing, 5–8
Charles Schwab Corporation, 116–117, 121
Chat room, online, 41, 136–137
Chick-fil-A, 116–117
Chief marketing officer, 105–106, 107–108
China, 6–7
Club Med, 121
Coca-Cola, 65, 94, 102
Communication skills
  customers and, 27, 32
  financial projections, 93, 101–102
  integrated marketing type, 118–119
  promotion allocations, 92, 96–101
  signs of problems with, 91
  solutions to problems with, 93
  target market and, 91
Competitors, defining and monitoring
  hiring employees from, 47–48
  intelligence on, 46, 47
  overfocus on wrong competitor, 45–46
  signs of problems with, 45

Competitors, defining and monitoring (*Continued*)
solutions for problems with, 46
value/price positions and, 49–51
Complaints, 32–33
Conjoint analysis, 39–40
Contact center, 27, 113–114
The Container Store, 116–117
Cross-selling, 84, 86–87
Culture of company, changing, 24–25
The Customer Comes Second (Rosenbluth), 24
Customer intimacy, 109–110
Customer orientation
employee organization and, 21–22
hierarchy of values and, 23–24
incentives and, 22–23, 24–26
signs of, 21
solutions for, 23
training and, 22
Customer Relationship Management
description of, 6, 111–112
software for, 41–42
Customers. *See* Research on customers; Target customers
Custom Research, 116–117

Dashboards, 132, 140–141
Database marketing, 111–112
Data warehouse, 41–42
Dealers. *See* Distributors
Dealing with sins, 9
Decision models, 132, 139
Dell Computer, 101, 115
Depth interviewing, 36, 38–39
Differentiation, 7
Direct marketing, 100–101
Disney, 94, 118
Disruptive technology, 48
Distributors
customers and, 26
management of, 60–61
panels of, establishing, 40–41
as stakeholders, 56
DuPont, 20, 79–80

Employees
customer satisfaction and, 25
e-recruitment, 135
hiring from competitors, 47–48
management of, 58–59
unhappy, signs of, 55
Employment, falling, 7
Engineering and marketing departments, 123–124
Enterprise Rent-A-Car, 116–117
E-procurement, 135–136
E-recruitment, 135
Ethnographic research, 40
E-training online, 135
Experiential marketing, 116–118
Extranets, 61, 134

The Fall of Advertising and the Rise of PR (Ries & Ries), 96, 116
FedEx, 121
Finance and marketing departments, 125–126
Financial projections, 93, 101–102
Focus
identifying segments and, 15–17
market segment managers and, 17–18
prioritizing segments and, 17, 19
segmentation techniques, 18–19

signs of, 15
solutions for, 18
verticalizing sales force, 20–21
Focus groups, 34–35
Ford, 108, 134

General Electric (GE), 49, 94, 109
General Motors, 97
Golin-Harris, 115

Haagen-Dazs, 51
Hamel, Gary, "Bringing Silicon Valley Inside Your Company," 67
Hard Rock Café, 117
Harley Davidson, 136–137
Harris, Tom, *A Marketer's Guide to Public Relations*, 115
Heinz, 86
Hiring from competitors, 47–48
Home Depot, 121

IBM, 19, 20, 47–48, 94, 135
Ideas, generating, 66–72
Identifying market segments, 15–17
IKEA, 121
Incentives
cross-selling and upselling, 87
customer service, 22–23, 24–26
In-home research, 36
In-store research, 37
Integrated marketing communications, 118–119
Intel, 94
Interbrand Corporation, 94
Internal marketing, 58–59
Internet marketing, 115, 131, 133–137
Intranet, 134
Investors, satisfaction of, 56–57

Johnson & Johnson, 24

Klein, Naomi, *No Logo*, 5–6
Kodak, 68
Kraft, 139

Laddering technique, 38–39
Lateral marketing, 71–72
Lexus, 51
Limited chain of stores, 16–17
Logistics and marketing departments, 126
Loyalty Rules (Reichheld), 57–58
Loyalty schemes, 6

Manufacturing and marketing departments, 124
Market-driving firm, 120–121
Market environment, 69
A Marketer's Guide to Public Relations (Harris), 115
Marketing mix modeling, 139
Marlboro, 94
Marriott Hotel chain, 24, 49–50
Mass marketing, costs of, 7
McDonald's, 94, 95, 109, 115–116
Measuring customer satisfaction, 25–26
Men and shopping, 37
Mercedes, 35, 51, 94
Microsoft, 94
Mossberg, Walter, 100
Mystery shopping, 37–38

Needs of customers, assessing, 38–39
Nestlé, 86

Nokia, 94
No Logo (Klein), 5–6

One-P marketing, 3–4
Online, buying, 8
Operational excellence, 109–110
Opportunities, finding new
  generating ideas, 69–72
  signs of problems with, 65–66
  solutions to problems with, 66
  stimulating ideas, 66–68
Organization of company
  chief marketing officer, 105–106, 107–108
  departmental relationships and, 106, 121–126
  marketing department, skills of, 106, 108
  signs of problems with, 105
  solutions to problems with, 107
Organization of employees, 21–22
Overfocusing on wrong competitor, 45–46

Panels of customers and dealers, establishing, 40–41
Partner relationship management, 112
Partners, stimulating ideas from, 66–68
Perceptual mapping, 39
Personal information, collection of, 6
Peters, Tom, 55
Phone support, 27, 113–114
Planet Hollywood, 117
Planning process
  celebration of, 79–80
  components of, 77–78
  flexible budgeting and, 78–79
  format of, 75–76
  signs of problems with, 75
  solutions to problems with, 77
Policies, product and service
  cross-selling and, 84, 86–87
  free services, 84, 86
  profitability and product proliferation, 83
  signs of problems with, 83
  solutions to problems with, 85
  tracking and evaluation system, 85–86
Positioning, 109–111
Positive-sum thinking, 57–58
Predictive analytics, 40
Preferences of customers, assessing, 39–40
Price consciousness, 8
Prioritizing market segments, 17
Problems with marketing, 3–5
Procter & Gamble (P&G), 65–66, 86
Product
  profitability and, 83
  returns of, 32–33
  tracking and evaluation system for, 85–86
Product leadership, 109–110
Profitability analysis, 83, 119–120
Public relations, 99–100, 115–116
Purchasing and marketing departments, 124–125

R&D and marketing departments, 123–124
Reichheld, Fred, *Loyalty Rules*, 57–58

Research, online, 136
Research on customers
analytical techniques, 38–40
depth interviewing, 36, 38–39
focus groups, 34–35
in-home, 36
in-store, 37
mystery shopping, 37–38
overview of, 34
surveys, 35–36
Returned merchandise, 32–33
Ries, Al and Laura, *The Fall of Advertising and the Rise of PR*, 96, 116
Ritz-Carlton, 26
Rosenbluth, Hal, *The Customer Comes Second*, 24

Sales and marketing departments, 122–123
Sales automation system, 131, 137–138
Sales force, verticalizing, 20–21
Sales lagging expectations, 32
Sales promotion, 98–99
SAP, 121
Segmentation of market
identifying, 15–17
manager of, 17–18
prioritizing, 17, 19
techniques for, 18–19
Service marketing, 116–118
Services, free, 84, 86
Situational analysis, 77
Software
Customer Relationship Management, 41–42
financial simulation, 76
market automation, 138–139
marketing automation, 132
sales automation system, 131, 137–138
Sony, 120, 133–134
Southwest Airlines, 51, 58, 107–108, 121
Stakeholder relationships
distributors, 56
employees, 55, 58–59
investors, 56–57
positive-sum thinking, 57–58
signs of problems with, 55
solutions to problems with, 57
suppliers, 55–56, 59–60
Starbucks, 95, 117, 121
Stimulating ideas from partners, 66–68
Stretch goals, 78
Suppliers, 55–56, 59–60
Surveys, 35–36
Swarovski, 50
Swatch, 121

Target customers
analytical techniques and, 38–40
data warehouse and, 41–42
panels, establishing, 40–41
research and, 34–38
returns, complaints, and, 32–33
sales, expectations, and, 32
signs of, 31
solutions for, 33
weak information and, 31–32
Technology, monitoring, 48–49
Technology, use of
dashboards, 132, 140–141
decision models, 132, 139
Internet, 131, 133–137
market automation, 138–139

Technology, use of (*Continued*)
sales automation system, 131, 137–138
signs of problems with, 131
solutions to problems with, 132
Telemarketing, 114
Telephone support, 27, 113–114
Ten Commandments of Marketing Effectiveness, 145–146
Ten Deadly Sins of Marketing, 10
3M Company, 65, 120
Tide, 51, 109
Tracking and evaluation system, 85–86
Training issues
cross-selling, upselling, and, 87
customer service and satisfaction, 22, 26
e-training online, 135
Transition zone, 37
Treacy, Michael, *The Value Disciplines of Market Leaders*, 109–110

Underhill, Paco, *Why We Buy: The Science of Shopping*, 37
Unilever, 85–86
Upselling, 87
USAA, 116–117

Valuation methods of brand equity, 94
The Value Disciplines of Market Leaders (Treacy & Wiersema), 109–110
Value/price positions, 49–51
Values for company, 23–24, 25
Verticalizing sales force, 20–21
Vertical marketing, 70–71
Virgin, 121
Volvo, 26, 100, 109

Wal-Mart, 26, 51, 95, 110, 121
Web site, 115, 131, 133–134
Why We Buy: The Science of Shopping (Underhill), 37
Wiersema, Fred, *The Value Disciplines of Market Leaders*, 109–110
W.W. Grainger, 115

Yield-based pricing, 138–139

Zero-sum thinking, 57